Mick Marc

DIMPLES TO WRINKLES
AND BEYOND

BY BILL PALMER

Published 2005 by arima publishing

www.arimapublishing.com

ISBN 1-84549-045-2

© Bill Palmer 2005

Printed and bound in the United Kingdom

Typeset in Garamond 11/20

arima publishing
ASK House, Northgate Avenue
Bury St Edmunds, Suffolk IP32 6BB
t: (+44) 01284 700321

www.arimapublishing.com

DEDICATION

I dedicate this book to Sheila the most understanding and loving wife in the world. Also to my three offspring Bernard, Billy and Debra, although not seeing much of their Dad (always out fishing) still turned out to be three lovely people.

ACKNOWLEDGEMENTS

I would like to take this opportunity to thank the bevy of beauties who helped with the typing of this book, Fran, Michelle, Carol and Yvonne. Special thanks go to Mick Toomer, Tony Corless, Steve Wells, Barry Summerhaye, Len Savage, Jeff Ducker, John Smith and Mem Hassan for the use of photographs, and finally a big thank you to Martin Gay for proof reading my manuscript.

CONTENTS

If readers of this book hope to find details of a secret method, or magic bait they will be disappointed. But if they are looking for the secret of success they will find it.

The 'secret' in pike fishing is in working hard, reading the water and the weather and correctly interpreting it, using tried and tested methods, baits that the pike want on the day and above all, above everything else, getting out there and fishing. Bill Palmer has this 'secret' and uses it with reverential success.

Without travelling huge distances, and certainly without the need to follow others to 'going' waters Bill has caught more large pike than almost any other angler in England yet he has done so in his typically quiet and unassuming way. Along that way he is probably the only angler in England to have a known 50 pound pike swirling in his swim and, but for a cruel turn of fate could so easily be the current record pike holder. The full story is told in this lovely book and after reading Bill's account, I cannot believe there will be any reader who does not feel for his plight and the anguish that consumed Bill during the days that followed the discovery of this huge fish.

My first meeting with Bill was in the 1970's on the banks of the King George V reservoir in Chingford, north London. A mutual friend, Peter Mann, took me along to share some of the fishing that he, Bill and other friends were enjoying at the time. I'm not sure to this day that these various friends 'thanked' Pete for doing this but I owe him a 'thank you' for introducing me to Bill, Len, and other lads whose names are mentioned in the following pages and whom I haven't seen for the best part of 20 years. Life runs by so quickly but it was though only yesterday when Bill contacted me for some information concerning Abberton reservoir, for his forthcoming book and I am only too delighted that we have made contact again.

Bill Palmer is not only what some people call a 'character' he is one of the most genuine anglers around and a role model for many of today's fishermen. His success, and not only with pike (his natural gift as an angler comes through in everything he does) will make your jaw drop as you read, and re-read this book. Take a tip from me and read between the lines for within those lines is all you need to know about pike yesterday, today and in the years ahead.

Martin Gay

I've pike fished all over the country, from big reservoirs and gravel pits, to the lochs of Scotland and Ireland, right down to small park lakes and tiny streams, though this book is mainly about just six periods in my life. My dimple years, the 'Big Pond', Abberton, trout water pike, my wrinkly years and beyond.

Covering nearly 50 years, the last 25 spent mainly fishing for pike, I've been very fortunate in that time to have over 200 twenty pounders grace my net.

Although I take my piking seriously, I do try not to lose sight that fishing is fun, in the bad times as well as the good.

In my early years I enjoyed all aspects of fishing. I couldn't get enough, from sticklebacks and newts to small rudd and perch. As a small boy I would paddle in the gravel runs of streams, lifting up the stones, fascinated by the bullheads and stone loach. In my teens, after joining the East Ham Angling Club I took an interest in match fishing. I loved to compete and match my skills against other anglers. In my twenties it was carp (as they became more wide spread) opening up the wonderful world of night fishing for me but all the time I would be thinking of pike fishing. 'Til then, in the late sixties, I reached a crossroads.

What path should I follow? Match fishing, carp or pike? No contest! Britain's number one predator won hands down.

Over the years I've been fortunate to have made some very good friends, their enthusiasm firing me up again and again, and one of them once asked me what was my greatest achievement in angling? No doubt about it, to see this book published. When I first told my mates I was writing a book they fell about laughing, maybe its the trouble I have speaking English let alone trying to write it, but you won't need a dictionary to find the meaning of any long words in this book, there aren't any. From Dimples to Wrinkles is my story.

1

THE DIMPLE YEARS AND ON...

I started fishing at the age of six, tagging along with my elder brother Brian, fishing the ponds at Wanstead. There was a sandpit on the Wanstead Flats, and just behind it there used to be a smaller pit, dug out I believe for sandbags during the war. It was full of junk, but held a small head of perch. I used the standard tackle for small boys, garden cane, catgut tied to the top, matchstick and eyed hook, bait was worm. I can still remember my first fish, after fishing for about an hour with no success, I was soon bored, and I was trying to catch a toad that was hiding between two oil drums. Meanwhile, my matchstick started to bob, I ran back to my cane, the gut was tight, and the matchstick is nowhere in sight. I lifted and out came a massive perch, all of 5"... that perch was going home!! I quickly put it in my large jar, to show mum and dad what a good fisherman I was! One scruffy, happy little boy was well and truly hooked. But I often wonder, if that little perch had not hung itself, whether I would still be fishing, nearly 50 years on?

The next few years found me fishing Wanstead Park boating lake, for roach. With our shoes and socks off, wading up to our bums, using breadcrust we put our floats right alongside the boats and as we stood there, gudgeon would bite our toes. Happy days! I teamed up with school mates, catching the train to Debden, to fish the River Roding, I learned how to stalk chub. All small boys should fish a river, a great place to learn. One of my school mates Ray Alexander (who is still a mate 50 years on, and still fishing with his Mk 4's) started to poach the Ornamental Waters in Wanstead Park, well not actually poach, we just avoided paying! It was a day ticket water, and at two shillings, there was no way I could afford to pay. With five brothers and a sister it was hard enough for mum and dad to put shoes on our feet! The water bailiff was forest ranger George, but more of George later. The water was full of islands and little bays set in the forest. A glade ran down to the water next to an old boat house (we used to call it the 'old castle'). The lake held a good head of roach, perch, tench and pike. And it was here that I caught my first pike, not one but two, 12 to 14 inch monsters, taking them on small roach in the lilies. I had to discard my jam jar for a 'wally tin', and the two pike were nose-to-tail in it. I had put them in the tin to show big brother Brian, who was fishing further round the lake. Brian soon appeared "What you caught Billy?" With a grin that must have gone all the way round my head, "Two absolutely huge pike", I say, "You little liar" he replied. I dragged the wally tin out from under a bush, Brian peered in. "There", I say, sticking out my chest. The poor pike were suffering from lack of oxygen, gulping down air they didn't look too good. "You'd better put them back" says Brian. "I'm going to, they'll be alright", says I, poking their heads down with my finger.... splash.... one angry pike is well and truly clamped to my hand!

I was doing a war dance, with all the vocals, trying to pull the pike off with the other hand. "Give us it here", says Brian, pulling the pike with all his might, only to remove the last bit of skin from my fingers.

Just then a man fishing nearby, hearing all the commotion, came to our rescue. "What's the matter boy?", he says, "A bloody big pike has hold of my brothers hand" shouted Brian. "Put the fish onto the ground and keep still", the man tells me, and with one swift movement he took the pikes head off with his sheath knife. There was no way I wanted that, after all, this was one of my first pike and all that was left was a head clamped on my fingers! Brian and I slowly opened the pike's jaws, and I noticed the hundreds of needle-like teeth, all sloping backwards. No wonder we had trouble trying to pull my hand out. I carefully removed my fingers, the rest of the day was spent at the hospital having my fingers treated and a rather unexpected jab in the backside!.

Two weeks later, I was back at the hospital again. Fishing the Ornamental Waters with Brian, with our rods strapped to the cross bars of our bikes, we raced round the lake to our favourite swims, weaving in and out of the trees. Around the edge of the lake, my little legs going like the clappers trying to keep up with Brian, suddenly my head was almost pulled from my shoulders, followed by a loud crack. The bike was all over the place and I was lucky to stay on. I put a hand to my head, to see what was causing the intense pain, but my hand became stuck fast. Taking my other hand off the handle bars something sharp pierced my hand and fingers, then my second hand became entangled with the first. The bike hit a tree root, and we parted and I splashed in to the lake, head first. Good job it was only two feet deep. I surfaced spitting out the water "Brian, Brian". Brian returned, seeing me in the water, and burst out laughing. "What are you doing in the water, and why are your hands on your head?". "They're stuck, I think I have a load of thorns in my head, Brian help me out", I say. He starts to pull at my head, I scream, "Shut up, its only a load of weed", he says. "Hang on, there's some cord, blimey its full of bloody great hooks". What had happened was some idiot, clearing a swim of weed, had put a dozen treble hooks on a length of cord, with an old sea weight on the end. He was swinging it round as I went by, and the whole shooting match had wrapped around my head.

Back at the hospital, the nurse removed most of my hair apart from a tuft or two, and freed one of my hands. In came the doctor "Don't worry son, we'll soon get rid of those horrible hooks", he said, as he examined my head. "Please mister, can I have the hooks when you get them out?", I asked.

The doctor looked at me amazed, "OK, I'll save what I can", he said as he went to work. Clink, the first treble hit the kidney dish, clink, two, three..... Two hours later, all patched up, Dad picked me up and we were on our way home. Clutched tightly in my better hand, were 7 blood stained trebles, rapped in cotton wool. This became my first ever pike tackle.

Things started to look up when I was given a 7 foot tank aerial with a cork handle, which with a small buckled brass centre pin reel, made up my tackle. Where the reel came from I cannot remember. In the year that followed I became quite good at taking pike from the surface, tempting them with livebaits as they basked in the sun.

At the time, with no piking experience, my ideal day for pike fishing would be hot and sunny, the hotter it was, the more pike would be on the surface. I would not actually fish unless I saw the pike first. I would ride round the lake, scanning the water, one eye checking the weed beds and under the trees, the other eye watching out for George.

One day as I searched out the water, by the 'old castle', my eyes caught sight of a large black shape, 40 yards out by an island. Surely that's not a pike, its got to be a log, its much too big, but my eyes nearly popped out as the 'log' slowly moved and sank from sight. Blimey, that pikes bigger than me. During the summer I saw the big one, lots of times, always in the same position, just off of the island, well out of my range.

But all that was about to change, for what was to happen next, would leave a lasting impression in my mind.

The day started like all the rest, arriving at the Ornamentals just as George started his rounds, I hid in the trees, and let George get a head start; I slowly follow him round. At the very first weed bed I spotted and landed my biggest pike to date, all of 5 pounds, wait 'till I tell Brian. I am still on cloud nine, as I reach the old castle, instantly my eyes look for the big one, but it was nowhere to be seen. Disappointed, I go to move on when I noticed something protruding from a small hole in the weed, only ten yards out. A closer inspection and my legs turn to jelly as a big head with cold eyes inched out into the hole, where some small roach played. It's the big one and in range. Would my tackle be up to the task? Hands shaking like mad, I lip hooked a roach on a treble, from the wally tin. A perch float made up the terminal tackle. The tackle was my pride and joy, the tank aerial, the buckled centre pin loaded with about 50 yards of assorted line that I had collected in small lengths from around the lake.

Shaking from head to foot, I cast the roach but the float landed on the weed just past the fish. I flicked the line, what luck, bait and float dropped in the hole, and the pike was still there. It seemed an eternity as I stand there, knees knocking together, heart beating faster and faster, but just when I thought my heart would burst, ... the big one strikes.

The perch float was gone, the line disappearing down into the hole, I sweep the rod back and all hell breaks out as I lose the handles of the reel, which is making a terrible noise. I hear the knots passing through the rings as the line is stripped from the reel, and the rod takes on an even more alarming curve as the line hit the stop knot at the reel. For a brief second, its tug of war between me and the fish. Finally, the knot gives, my hand is snatching at the last of the line as it disappears up the rod into the water. The big one is gone. I sink to my knees, tears filling my eyes, but a determination comes over me. One day!

For the next year or two, I'm content to fish my local ponds, catching pike to just under double figures. I learned the 'lift' method, catching bags of tench using peacock quill and flake. Fishing the Ornamentals, I often saw George, him on one side of the lake, me on the other; as we pass, I wave a hand, he waves a fist! George, at six foot plus is impressive in his forest ranger's uniform, riding boots, and mounties hat!!

The day of long trousers, work arrives and I'm employed by 'Art-Wallpapers' in East Ham, at the age of 15. Now I am rich at £2 10 shillings a week, the sky's the limit. Girls, clothes, expensive tackle, whoops sorry .... expensive tackle, clothes, girls!!!

Mum soon brought me back to earth with a bump, with £2 going towards my keep I'm left with the 10 shillings, though still a small fortune! Working a 5 1/2 day week interfered with my fishing and I was only able to go on Sundays.

After my first week's work, I'm back at the Ornamentals fishing for roach with hemp seed, just off the path behind some rhododendrons. Suddenly I here footsteps on the gravel, crunch, crunch. It's George! his riding boots giving him away. Normally I would be well gone, slipping away before George reached me, but with silver in my pocket, I decided to pay. Crunch, crunch, crunch, half a dozen quick steps and he's behind me in the rhododendrons. All goes quiet, I was just about to turn around, when this 'mad bull' came raging through the rhododendrons. Flowers and leaves going everywhere, arms outstretched, he grabs my collar. "Got you, I've bloody well got you", George cries, I say "I would have been on my bike long ago, but I've started work, I can afford to pay", pulling some silver out of my pocket.

"Pay, you're going to pay?", said George "after all these years you're going to pay". A big grin came over his face "put your money away, pay me some other day". We shook hands, lovely old George!

After a few weeks working for Art-Wallpapers, my old school mate, Ray Alexander, told me of a vacancy where he worked. The job was at Catering Bros, who were a grocery firm, and were paying £4 10 shillings, £2 more than I was earning. I jumped at the chance. Teamed up with Ray again, we joined the East Ham A.S. as juniors. The idea being, with no transport of our own, bikes apart, the club would take us all over the country to all sorts of rivers and lakes.

The club held weekly meetings at the Earl of Wakefield in East Ham. We had to be proposed and seconded. Ray's next door neighbour was a member of the club, and took us for our first meeting. The club rented a large room above the pub, and as we entered I was taken in by the large number of cased fish around the room. Roach over 2lbs, tench to 5 1/4lbs, a brace of big perch, a large dace, monster pike, "monster pike"! My eyes stop, with mouth agape I just stare. 15¼lbs, the most impressive fish I had ever seen, a real man's fish. "Bill, Bill", Ray shaking my arm, "sit down, the meetings about to start".

The club was affiliated to the London Anglers Association, and held two matches a month. The venues of which were voted for by the members, the week before. In the years that followed I fished most, if not all, the rivers in the southern England. I was getting quite good at this match fishing lark, though mind you, the club charged 10 shillings a trip, with a shilling pool, plus bait, I had to win to keep afloat! The week between matches, Ray and I would fish for bigger fish, catching the Stratford Flyer to the River Lea. Wherever I went, my pike tackle went too, using it at every opportunity.

It was in the Lea Valley, I caught my first doubles, in the "Met" and "Police Pit" on livebaits. 'Til now I don't think I'd seen another pike angler, other than the roach angler with bung and billiard cue, which was put out when a pike attacked his swim. Looking back, at that moment in time, I don't think I actually saw another angler deliberately fishing just for pike. Even so my pike fishing was taking a back seat as I had my match fishing head on. I was enjoying the friendly, but fierce competition.

Meanwhile, back at work, a young lady started. "What's your name darling", I ask. "Sheila" she replied, fluttering her eye lashes. Within four years, Sheila was to become my bride.

I'm 17 years old now, had purchased a second hand motor bike, a BSA 250 and with my sheepskin flying jacket, I'm the bees knees. With my new found independence, that the bike brought, Sheila and I started to explore new and exciting waters. I discovered carp fishing. Up to then the only carp I had seen was a fish from the Ornamental Waters. An angler fishing at the glade had quite a crowd around him peering at the fish, a 'common' of about 3lbs. He was telling the crowd the carp must be 200 years old. A carp in the early 50's was a very rare creature indeed. A friend told of a gravel pit at Dagenham (Bent Marshals), holding a good head of 'wildies' up to 6lbs. Brian, Ray and I began to fish there on a regular basis, using 'modern' bite indicators, clothes pegs, lights, candle-in-a-jar. Bait was floating crust, on which we caught carp to 5lbs in weight. It was at Bent Marshals that I was to learn a very important lesson, one that would prove most valuable in years to come. The standard method at the pit was to cast as far as you could towards the middle, allowing the crust to rise to the surface, letting the line run through the swivel that was attached to a 3 ft tail holding a 1oz lead. The rod was then placed on rests and the clothes peg clipped on. If you weren't watching your indicators, I mean "pegs" when a carp took the bait, you were alerted by the sound of the peg hitting the rod, and you had to grab it, before it took off.

I suppose it was an early type of bolt rig fishing but, back to the lesson learned..... I was night fishing, and had cast my crust to the horizon. On tightening down, the line became snagged, and as I pulled for a break, the line parted at the reel. I was left with only about 15 yards of line! I decide to fish on, dropping my bait just off the rod-top. A good nights fishing at Bent Marshals would be about 6 fish to 4lbs, but only able to fish the margins, I went on to catch 20 carp to 6lbs, a lesson I was glad to learn. It was here at Bent Marshals also, that Sheila went on her first and last night fishing trip. What a disaster! I told Sheila to wrap up warm, as it got cold at night, but on picking her up she was wearing a thin blouse, trousers, and slip-on shoes, "Oh well"! As the night wore on, and with two carp landed the temperature started to drop and as I concentrated on my pegs I heard a strange noise behind me. It was Sheila, tucked up in a ball, teeth chattering like mad and stuck on her feet were my gloves! As dawn came Sheila decided to make breakfast, to keep warm. Using my stove, the smell of eggs and burgers filled the air. That's not the only thing to fill the air, as the sky blackened, the heavens opened.... Sheila tripped over, kicking the stove over as she hit the mud. Two burgers go floating past me and Sheila clawed her way up the bank! Grabbing her hand, we ran to a hut near the gravel workings. I went back to check the tackle and on returning to the hut with the rain subsiding, and the sun starting to peep through, "Come on Sheila, lets go back to the fishing", I say, as I open the door. Standing there covered in mud, her hair ringing wet, with tears streaming down her cheeks, "I want to go home", she cries. Soon after, Sheila and I were engaged and with my new responsibilities, I made a start with Advance Laundries, at Manor Park. It was about this time, I did my Barry Sheen act...... I was going for my copy of the Angling Times at the confectioner but was stopped by the traffic lights, at Manor Park Broadway. As the lights changed, I grabbed the throttle and with front wheel off the ground, I'm across the lights. As I pass the wet fish shop, (it had to be a fish shop) a (f*****) motorist decided to open his door, my left hand and leg made contact, taking the door off it's hinges. Doing a triple somersault through the air I hit the road a split second before the bike, that had been following me. As I lay there dazed, I heard the sound of screeching brakes, and the smell of burning rubber. Thud! Something hard hit the back of my head, as I look up, there was a bloody great bus! I'd only gone to get my Angling Times, this fishing lark is getting dangerous! Two weeks later, and out of hospital, the club was fishing a match at East Peckham, on the River Medway. With a broken leg and hand, stitches in my head, a little thing like this won't stop me!

The coach picked me up at home, and arriving at the venue it was raining. In fact it had been raining all night, the banks were covered in liquid mud. At the call off, most members went right. I go left and with my leg in plaster from my ankle to the top of my thigh, it's slow going. I pass the last of our members as I made for a good dace swim 30 yards on, round a bend. The rain was coming down harder as I reached the swim. I let the tackle drop to the ground and I take a well earned rest. Big mistake. As I attempted to reach the waters edge, my legs would not move and, looking down I'd sunk past my ankles. Grabbing the rod handle with my good hand, I tried to lever myself out. The more I struggled the deeper I sank, half hour later I'm up to my knees. After 45 minutes I gave up, the plaster cast on my leg seemed to be dragging me down. The rain was pouring down my neck, "Please somebody help me", I shout. Four hours later a passing angler found me, now down to my waist, and, with the help of three others, they haul me out. To say I was a keen fisherman was an under-statement, I was obsessed!!

It was later that year, fishing with the club on the Suffolk Stour I was to come upon the biggest concentration of pike I'd ever seen. It was the last month of the season in early March and after fishing hard for two hours, I hadn't had a sniff. I decided to rest the swim and go walkies, checking members as I go, to see if anyone's catching. It's the same story, returning to my swim, I give it another half hour... I blank, it seems the river is void of fish. With the three month close season staring me in the face, I was desperate to catch a fish or two. Packing away my match gear, I took out my Mk 4, on the reel goes the spool with 10lb line and with a box of spinners, net and some odd's and end's, I was off down the river. I'll just winkle a pike out before I go home, me thinks!

For the first hour, working my spinner in all the likely spots, deep holes, slacks, slow glides, not a sausage! I'd covered about a mile, using my massive collection of lures (3!) I'm about to call it a day, but in the distance, I saw an L.A.A. notice board. After walking all this way, I decided to fish, on up to the end of the fishery. I cast the spinner to the far side of the river, dropping it a foot from the far bank. With one turn of the reel the rod goes over. "Sod it", I say, thinking I've snagged, the rod kicks, "you jammy begger Bill", I shout as I play the fish to hand. A pike of about 6lbs, and I'm very pleased to see it. Unhooking the fish, I recast the spinner to the same spot, three turns of the handle, the rod slams down again another fish about the same size as the first. On my third cast, the spinner reached the middle, and I can see it two feet under the surface. With a flash, it's engulfed by three feet of yellow, a fish of 11lbs. I move on 5 yards, 3 more casts, 3 more fish, it's really happening! I've just covered a mile of river, without a touch, yet my last 6 casts produced 6 fish. Surely this can't go on, but it did, every cast resulting in a fish. I started to work the spinner just under the surface, the pike were popping up from the decaying weed, and homing in on it.

As I retrieve the lure the pike are coming from all angles up to three at a time. I'm speeding the spinner, taking it out of the mouth of one fish, as a bigger one moves in. After three hours of non-stop action I collapsed to the ground exhausted, hardly able to move my arms. How many fish I caught I don't know, but they averaged about 6lbs with 5 low doubles. Probably the only time in my life, I didn't want to catch another fish! It seemed the entire pike population of the River Stour had moved into that small 100 yard stretch, prior to spawning.

As I start to make my way back, one of the members, Peter Jackson, greets me, "Had any Bill" asked Peter. "You wouldn't believe it" I say, thrusting my rod in his hand, "come on Pete, catch yourself a pike". "Where shall I cast Bill", asked Peter, "Anywhere you like I say!". Peter sends the lure straight down the river. Half a dozen turns of the handle the rod goes over. "Jeronimo" screams Peter, as a 3lb jack leaps two feet into the air. His first ever pike. Ten fish later I had to prise the rod from his hands. Looking at my watch, "Come on Peter, we will be late back for the coach".

With almost 50 years of fishing behind me, I've never again come across so many fish in such a small area. I wonder what weight a modern young gun would have amassed, fishing all day, given the same circumstances?

The 'Big Pond' was a big reservoir at Ponders End. It was another one of the London Anglers waters and to gain entry you had to purchase a key from the club. We were drawn there by talk of huge shoals of big perch. I'll never forget my first day on the water. Locking the gate behind me, I climbed the 30 steps to the top of the reservoir's bank. Greeting me was the biggest sheet of water I had fished to date - 5 miles of bank with a depth averaging over 20 feet.

Two steps down off the wall there is a brick bank, gently sloping to the waters edge. Walking a few yards with my Polaroids on, it was like looking into a massive fish tank, roach and perch fry darting in and out of the weed in the gin clear water. A gentle breeze was coming off the east wall as I made my way around the reservoir. I was casting my Devon Minnow into a giant mirror only broken as the lure hit the water. As it bumps up the slope, it was attacked by tiny 2" perch half the size of the bait practising for when they are bigger.

I'd covered about 250 yards when a decent fish swirled 30 yards further on, two more hit the top as I wind up fast so I can cover the fish. As I run along the bank big fish were everywhere, thousands of fry were leaping clear of the water and as they fell back it was like showers of rain followed by hundreds of big spiked dorsals. The perch were driving the fry right up the bank and as I stood there the fish were flapping around my feet, perch half beaching themselves as they snapped away. What an incredible sight! The water was almost boiling now as I cast to the mass of fish, landing three in quick succession. It was all over in minutes, the perch moving out to deeper water.

Ray, John Meecham, another old school mate, and I, hit the water hard that season. Taking up to 10 fish each in a session averaging 11/2lbs, with the odd fish going over 2lbs. Using minnows collected in traps from the River Roding at Debden, we often ran out of bait. As I learned more about the reservoir a hot spot was found. Half way round there is a breakwater about 10 feet across, running from one side of the reservoir to the other. As we slowly worked our baits along the breakwater we found, on reaching the middle, that takes increased; passing on towards the other bank they decreased. There was definitely some sort of holding area dead centre of the two halves of the reservoir. Fishing the hot spot for the perch with 6lb line, a number 6 hook tied direct, striking the odd run a bite off would result. Landing an 8lb pike early on, I put it down to small pike...... what a plonker! Back in the club room, we quizzed Ted Cole about his brace of big perch on the club wall, taken at Enfield. Telling him of our exploits on the reservoir, he assured us he had his perch from the Lea, but he can remember fishing the reservoir a few years back with his uncle Sep. On arriving they found the level right down to the gravel and walking along the ledge they found lost leads and lures from years before. On reaching the centre, with the low water a

A perch from the 'Big Pond', yet it was 10 years before the penny dropped about the pike potential!

Just one of the huge number of pike I caught on the Stour.

culvert was exposed 20 feet wide running out from both sides of the wall. Ted cast a small spinner into it and hooked a 11/2lb perch. As he played it, a great pike as big as a railway sleeper came up and took it, smashing his line like cotton, he said. Tackling up again he recast hooking into another perch. As the fish surfaced at the edge of the culvert Ted bent down to pick it out. Ted said "As I reached out staring up at me was this crocodile two feet from my perch. I turned to stone as the pike engulfed the 2lb fish, biting through my line then slowly sinking back down into the culvert". We fell about laughing pulling silly faces, "railway sleepers, crocodiles, what were you drinking Ted?", we say.

Oh foolish one, non-believer, man with no brain, obviously Ted had exaggerated a bit, but the penny still hadn't dropped! What a 'dick-head' I was, it was nearly ten years later before the penny did finally drop and I returned.

Meanwhile, I was still engrossed in my match fishing, all my waking hours taken up with it. Come to think of it, so were my sleeping hours too! In my dreams I would actually fish the match the night before.

There was one dream I can remember to this day. The match was to be held on the River Beane at Hertford, the water was gin clear with streamer weed, but it all got mixed up with my work. I was foreman at the laundry now, and we were having a lot of claims for damaged shirts and I was given the job to eliminate it. What was happening with 500 shirts in the machine was that by the time the process ended, they were in one gigantic knotted ball and the operator was pulling the odd sleeve off when he tried to untangle them. So I brought in some nylon nets, they were just like keepnets, without the rings. Putting 50 shirts in each one doing the net up with a large pin, the damage was eliminated. The only trouble was, with the restricted movement, the real grubby shirts, especially collars and cuffs would not be cleaned.

The week leading up to the match found me at work with a scrubbing board, brush and a jug of liquid soap, scrubbing each collar and cuff before dropping the shirts into the nets, the majority being Van Heusens. The night before the match arrived, and my brain in overdrive, I climbed into bed. I'm going over and over the match in my mind, and thinking what a poxy week I'd had at work, with all that scrubbing. Finally I slipped into the land of nod. Before the first zed hit the air, I'm at the draw my number called out and I'm off down the river. I'd got the swim I wanted, on the bend with the water cutting into my bank giving me a 20 yard run between streamer weed. First things first, grabbing a handful of mud from the river bank I rub it onto my hands. Taking out the bait tin, in goes two handfuls of hemp and one of maggots, at the head of the swim. My 14 foot match rod is soon assembled and I'm trotting my float down the 4 foot deep swim. Third trot down the float dipped, I struck and something heavy tried to get under the weed, I applied side strain slowly gaining line. I got a glimpse of it as I lowered the landing net, just as I thought of a Van Heusen, its sleeves trying to lock onto the weed, the shirt tail twisting in the current. Its in the net and I lift. Unhooking it I place the collar onto my measuring board, 13" its a goer! Dropping it into the keepnet 5 more Van Heusens join it in the net. Two more handfuls of hemp and maggots go into the swim. Next trot down the float cuts across the flow, I strike, the shirt's darting from side to side as it goes over the landing net, I see the 'slim lines'...... No, it can't be, yes its a Ben Sherman, a rare shirt for this stretch! The Van Heusens moved back in and my keepnet is almost full! As the match draws to a close, I have one final trot down, the float reaching the very end of the swim. I hold it back, it sinks down, the rod goes over and starts tapping away. The shirt's dancing all over the river, I might have guessed a Raelbrook.

I pack up and try to lift my keepnet from the river, it won't move. I'm straining every muscle in my body. Suddenly there's a ringing in my ears, I awake to the sound of my alarm clock, in a cold sweat, on the morning of the real match!

I know I should be certified, but the dream was so real and to think I hadn't started my serious pike fishing yet!

Talking about certified, what about superstition? Did not the great Dick Walker say, "If you see a magpie when going fishing, tip your hat", saying "good morning Mr Magpie"? Well whatever King Dick said was law, and for the last 30 years, its been "good morning", "afternoon" and "night Mr Magpie!"

Meanwhile, Sheila and I are married, a year later our first son is born, Bernard, named after (Mr Crabtree himself) Bernard Venables. What an inspiration he was to all boys, big and small.

I'm still enjoying my match fishing winning many cups and trophies. The specimen hunting was going quite well with pike up to 20lbs from the "valley", and a couple of 20lb carp from Brooklands in Kent. In the late 60's at the club's annual dinner and dance, I took home 80% of the trophies we fished for one year. When the last cup was presented, Sheila was called up to the table by the club chairman, and given a large box. Returning back to our table she was asked to open it, almost dying with embarrassment, she pulled out a gallon tin of Blue Bell (metal polish).It seemed I had gone as far as I could with the club, and the challenge had gone. After many happy years, Ray and I reluctantly resigned giving us the opportunity for more time to put one or two bigger specimens on to the bank. That summer most weekends would find me camped at Horton Kirby, or at Brooklands for the carp.

As winter arrived, my thoughts turned to pike, but where to fish? Looking at my Ordnance Survey map of the Lea Valley, checking out lakes and pits my eyes caught sight of the big reservoir at Ponders End, and my mind went back to the time when we fished there for perch before the disease. Christ what a fool I was, railway sleepers, crocodiles, isn't that what Ted had told us? I couldn't wait to get back there. A trip was arranged for the coming Saturday with a work mate, Bob Slaughter. Ray was working and couldn't make it. I picked Bob up and we arrived at Ponders End, just as dawn broke, parking the car by the bridge that crossed the Lea.

The plan was to knock out a dozen baits in the first hour, then to the reservoir for the pike. Four hours later with three small roach and six bleak (you can never catch bait when you want to, can you!) we made our way round the reservoir to the centre. The wind was coming through from the north so we planned to fish the south half, Bob fishing on the right of the centre, me on the left. The reservoir's rules were one rod only and as I hadn't been lead astray yet, it was one rod we fished. The rod was a Mk 4, 10lb line, a running lead, 18 inch trace with a number 6 treble. I lip hooked a small roach and cast it 40 yards out, clipping on a washing up bottle top, opened the pick up and sat back against the wall to wait.

Half an hour passed, my eyes searching along the walls of the reservoir for the other anglers, but I guess Bob and I are the only ones there. "Bill" Bob shouts, my eyes instantly going to my rod, the washing up bottle top hits the bottom ring then drops to the ground and starts to jump up and down. Picking the rod up the line was pouring from the spool. Unclipping the bobbin I felt the fish as the line pulled between my fingers. What a wonderful feeling that is, the run being a big part of pike fishing, a jack, a "lump", the unknown.

I wound down to the fish and pulled the rod back, which went over and stayed there as a good fish moved off. The fish hugged the bottom for a

The 'Big Pond' and what a start! Three big doubles on the first trip.

My first 'Big Pond' twenty.

minute or two, I put on more pressure and it surfaced. Bob netted it first go. I could hardly stand as my legs were shaking so much. The fish weighed 15½ lbs, not a railway sleeper or a crocodile, but a beautifully marked fish, and a good start!

Before I recast Bob was away, the fish again kept deep, I did the honours with the net, Bob's fish also going 15lb. An hour later, I was away again with a fish of 14½ lbs. What a start to our first session on the 'Big Pond' with three mid-doubles.

So began my love affair with the big reservoir at Ponders End......an affair that was to last five years......

2

THE BIG POND

The 'Big Pond' was probably one of the best kept secrets in the early seventies and which at that moment in time must have been one of the top pike waters in our part of the country. But before I could write about the 'Big Pond', I had to find the friends I fished there with 25 years ago, because there was no way I would do this chapter without their consent.

I was still in contact with Colin Benbrook, but had lost touch with Len Savage and Jeff Ducker, who had moved over to the carp scene. Colin finally got hold of Jeff's phone number, and a meeting was arranged at a working mans club at Ilford. Steve Wells and Tony Corless asked if it would be okay to tag along, so picking them up with Colin, armed with pen, paper and a dictaphone, I headed for Ilford.

Greeting the lads, I introduced Steve and Tony, with a few pints down our necks we started the meeting. Now, knowing the lads as I do, I asked a dozen quick questions before the hard drinking began and the stories started to flow.

Steve turned on the dictaphone and placed it on the table.

"Right, first of all, do you mind me naming the 'Big Pond'?

Len "No, it don't apply now".

Jeff "What the carp fishery?".

Colin, "Well yeah".

(now Colin won't even tell his wife what he catches, but he wants to be famous, so he gives in). Len, "Jeff's right, its basically a carp water now, Colin".

"Right, so you don't mind me naming the King George Reservoir, blimey

I'm still having trouble actually naming it now, it must have been the best kept secret in our time up there".

Jeff, "Yeah that's when people could keep a secret Bill".

"I suppose that's why we called it the 'Big Pond', so when we talked about our time there we did not give it away".

Len, "It was actually Peter Mann who named it the 'Big Pond'".

Jeff, "Whatever happened to Peter?" (Peter used to run the Home Counties Specimen Group).

Len, "I believe he became a cab driver and went completely bald".

Colin, "He didn't have a lot of hair in the first place".

"The date we all met up at the Big Pond, who was fishing up there at the time? I know Peter Mann was and one or two of his group, Ray Taylor and, who else Len?"

Len, "Dave Wilson and Tony Galloway".

"Cor blimey yeah, Tony Galloway, he was a nice bloke."

Len, "Me and Terry started in 1969, Bill started a year or two later, Jeff in 1970 or '71.

"So you came up in 1971 Jeff, what did you think of us?"

Jeff, "I liked you Bill (creep), I tell you what happened I came up with Dicky Doser".

"I remember you coming Jeff, looking like that strange bloke, cat weasel".

Jeff "Looking at the old photos, I now know why Bill".

Colin, "It was them skin tight trousers and long socks you wore Jeff".

Bill, "How did you come to hear about the 'George, Jeff?"

Jeff, "Pete Olley told me". We crept up in the corner first, then gradually nearer and nearer to you, it was a year and a half before I got my first run, then I missed the bugger".

Bill, "Who was it that started the tagging up there, it was you, wasn't it Len?"

Len, "Yeah, Terry and I".

"How many twenties do you reckon the 'George had? That goes to all three of you"

Jeff, "Well I caught 16 different twenties".

Bill, "I believe we thought there were about 40 at the time, but I reckon we over estimated it".

Len, "I think you were talking of about 25, I don't think there were any more than that".

Bill, "At the very beginning when I first fished there, and before the tagging, we said there were 20 twenties then we upped that to 40, I believe if we split that down the middle we wouldn't be far out. There are always some you don't catch".

Bill, "Then there was the south half, it didn't get as much pressure as the north. There were probably holding areas where the pike didn't move far, and we never found them. So we agree a population of between 25 to 30 twenties, yeah?

When did you start fishing the George, Colin?"

"1972".

Len, "You came up with the Brownies didn't you Colin?"

Jeff, "I remember you coming up, you were 28, I was there when you had your first twenty".

Len, "He's always been 28".

Jeff, "Yeah, like Bill he's always been 33".

" OK, OK, lets go on to rigs. Now this book's not going to be about rigs, but there were some interesting ones started there, so let's get it right on who started what. Who was it, who first started the poly baits, Colin?"

Len, "No I started that".

Colin, "I'm one down already, I'm never going to be famous!"

Len, "I started to use polystyrene to lift my deadbaits up out of the silk weed, that's before we started to inject them with air. What was happening, I was fishing the 'George with Dave Wilson and Tony Galloway and every time we reeled in, the baits were covered in silk weed, so I wired a chip of polystyrene to the bait. Dave Wilson said that's not nice, you could leave a piece of poly and wire in a fish, so I started to stitch the polystyrene on. Then someone come up with a hypodermic syringe and we started to pump the baits up".

"So who was it then who first started air injected baits on the 'George. I do remember reading in Angling Times some bloke had a 25lb fish on a small bream injected with air, this was in the late sixties".

Len, "I believe it was Wagstaffe who first wrote about it, the first time I heard about it was that some guy in the early 60's was injecting lob worms".

"If your life depended on catching a pike what rig would you use?"

Jeff, "The 'dead-and-alive' ".

Bill, "Although that's a good rig, a poly'd livebait is the one, over the

31

years it's caught me a lot of fish. A small livebait on a no.1 single hook with a piece of poly wired to the eye of the hook, the bait tethered 18" off the bottom - it works like hell. Anyway, as for air injected baits, although it was used before our time at the 'George, I believe our exploits there brought it to the fore".

Len, "Yes that's right Bill, Terry and I even used it in the Met in the 60's, again to beat the silk weed".

"I mucked about with a 'dead-and-live' bait rig, basically it was the same as the poly-live, the only difference being, instead of having poly on, you would inject a small deadbait with air and put it on the top hook of your trace and a small livebait on the second hook. The air injected deadbait would keep the livebait off the bottom, the livebait keeping both baits working without them becoming masked in weed. As for the slow sinker, that come about one day when a big fish struck on the surface, quite a rare thing for the 'George. That day I was fishing air injected roach of about 8ozs ledgered with a 11/2oz lead. I had clipped on a swan shot as a stop to the lead so I could fish the bait at different depths off the bottom. I wound the bait in to cast to the fish, and just as I was about to let fly, I decided the fish might still be high in the water, so I unclipped the lead and cast, the bait hit the surface and stayed there, being full of air. I wound in and gently squeezed out a little air, then tested it in the water.

The swan shot up-ended the bait, and it started to sink very, very slowly, I then cast to the fish. The bait was only half way down in 20ft of water when it was taken and the slow sinker was born. It was to become a very successful method for me, especially in deep clear gravel pits and reservoirs, like the 'George. Who started the plastic indicator clips?"

Len, "That was me".

Jeff, "Everything that was invented there was Len's, can I have one Len?"

Colin, "You've got no chance".

Len, "I've still got the original one with the same elastic band, I've also still got the patent somewhere indoors".

"I'm still using them now and again".

Jeff, "I know what Colin invented! He invented "sharpen your trebles too much so you keep losing fish, that's what he taught me!"

Colin, "Or they snapped!"

Jeff, "Yeah, when you were using the postman's string".

"Come on lads what other rigs did we have then?"

Len Savage (top) and Jeff Ducker with two fine mid-twenties from the 'Big Pond'.

Two fish caught simultaneously.

Releasing a 24³ᐟ⁴ pounder.

Jeff, "We used the simulated deadbait rig, putting Alka Seltzer tablets in the deadbait. As the gas built up the bait would rise then fall".

"I can remember having a discussion about the middle cut rig, that was something to do with Len wasn't it?"

Len, "Yeah the old John West".

Colin, "I've got another one, what about the old plum duff. I bet that's not going in the book. The old plum duff rig!"

"Come on Len give us the story about the plum duff rig".

Len, "I minced up some fish and put it in a piece of muslin, tying it up with an elastic band with a large single hook set on the side of the bag, I had a run on it too!"

"We're laughing but Len might have something there. Look at all the big pike coming out on fish meal boilies now".

Anyway, I better go back to the story, the boys have given this chapter their blessing, the meeting was getting out of hand, so I will just refer to some of the more printable stories later in the chapter.

Right where was I? Oh yeah, Bob and I had our first pike trip to the 'George landing 3 doubles and I couldn't wait to get back there. I told Ray about the fish Bob and I had and he decided he was coming on the next trip. He wasn't that impressed and I had to twist his arm. Ray was never really into pike fishing, I think it was only the curiosity of it that he agreed to come at all. Again, catching a dozen small roach and bleak from the Lea, Ray and I headed for the centre but on arriving we found it occupied, one angler fishing the south half one the north, the anglers being Len and Terry Savage.

Ray and I decide to fish the north half, we positioned ourselves about 20 yards to the right of the centre of the reservoir. I had fitted up and cast a bait out in one minute flat, Ray was still tarting about and it was 15 minutes later before he finally hooked on a small roach and dropped it 20 yards out on his Mk 4 Avon. Yes, you have guessed it, half an hour later Ray's washing up bottle top took off. With a bit of advice from me he wound down to the fish and struck.

His Avon nearly bent double as the pike went on its first powerful run. Three more runs and with the pike finally beaten Ray drew it over the waiting net, and I lift it out of the water and up on top of the wall. Len placed the fish onto a weighing net, hooked in a spring balance and lifted 20lbs 8ozs. Up on to the wall, the net unfolded and there before me was this beautiful creature, the yellows and oranges, the greens, what a wonderful fish, I believe

Ray was quite pleased too!

I would have sold my soul to the devil to swap places with Ray that day, and do you know that was to be Ray's first and last pike trip, he hasn't pike fished since! It was just as well I hung on to my soul, for in the month that followed I went on to beat my personal best pike three times to a weight of 26lbs 4ozs.

Len and Terry had befriended me and two very experienced and inventive anglers they were. Both being tool makers, Terry made me my first large landing net, with an aluminium spreader block and glass arms. You couldn't buy that in a tackle shop in those days. They even built left hand multipliers from scratch, the only ones on the market at the time being right hand ones. I remember the day when I had the 26lb 4oz fish, my first pike over 25lbs.

I arrived at the reservoir while it was still dark. Parking the car my watch read 6.00 o'clock. I started the mile and a bit walk to the centre, walking faster and faster as I approached. Taking out a pack of frozen rudd I dropped them into the water to thaw. Looking around I was pleased to be the first one there, my rods were soon assembled, with a rudd of about 4ozs mounted onto the trace with two no.6 trebles. A couple of swan shots added, I injected the bait and pumped in some air. Checking the bait sinks, I cast out, and put the rod in the rests.

On the other rod was an air injected bleak, cast about 15 yards to the right of the rudd. Putting a strip of silver paper round the line, I clipped it back on the rod rest. Ten minutes pass, I started to twitch the rudd back very slowly, second twitch something twitches back, the line tightens and starts to uncoil from the spool as a fish moves off. Pulling into the fish I had to backwind from the off, the fish felt heavy so I take my time. Working the fish away from the centre, after two more powerful runs she surfaced and I inch her to the net. On seeing her size, the trembling in my legs that's been there from the start of the fight starts to travel through my body down my arm holding the landing net. I didn't seem to have any control at all. After two or three frantic attempts, I finally rolled her in the net and with her safely enmeshed, I stood there gibbering. I was in no state to unhook or weigh the fish, so I bit through the line and transferred the fish to my large hessian sack. Safely sacked up, I slumped back against the wall, just as the silver paper flew off my second rod. Back on my feet and over to the rod in one movement, instantly winding down on the fish. After a brief struggle a big double graced my net, the single hook just inside the mouth. I remove it with my extended long nose pliers, (I didn't possess artery forceps then), and placed it in the sack alongside the bigger fish. With both rods out of the water, I poured myself a cup of tea, wishing I had something a wee bit stronger. As I climbed up onto the wall, I noticed three of the lads making their way down to the centre. Five minutes later Len, Terry and Ray Taylor arrived. The smaller fish weighed 17½ lbs. We then removed the trace from the bigger fish and placed it in the weigh net. I hook in the Avons and lifted 26lbs 4ozs. Yes, yes. It was three days before I finally came back down from the clouds. Recalling this story, I am reminded of the big hessian sacks we used in those far off days. What a difference from the modern keep sacks; you can wring them out and fold them away to nothing. The big hessian sacks weighed a ton when wet, but they did have their advantages. You could fold it over a couple times using it as a cushion keeping your bum off the cold brick bank, it also doubled as a blanket wrapping it around ourselves to keep warm. That first season at the 'George I landed 20 odd pike, the average weight being 18¼ lbs, I believe Len and Terry enjoyed similar success. Len used to keep a record of all the pike we caught, recording the weights on the back of his cigarette packets, then transferring them when he arrived home. He said it worked out that every third fish was a twenty, it was just like being in heaven, from struggling to catch say 10 doubles a season, I was in with a real chance of 10 twenties!

In the late 60's early 70's, we were just looking for a water that might produce a twenty, not like today when every pit and pond seems to have them. We did not even talk about thirties, that was something you only dreamed about. Anyway it seemed there were no small pike in the reservoir at all.

We believe it was probably due to the steep sides of the reservoir, the pike having trouble spawning. What with the perch disease, the pike's main food gone, when the pike did spawn their offspring were soon mopped up. In the early days there were about six hard core anglers there, with the odd angler turning up from time to time fishing once or twice, then not to be seen again. It was all so friendly, the hotspot being able to accommodate about 12 rods, six rods in the south half, six in the north all the rods being fished around the culvert. Fishing only one rod there was plenty of room, only when everybody had got their first rod out did one or two of us fish a second, fishing it 20 or 30 yards along the bank.

If you were first there with two rods out, and another angler turned up you would automatically take a rod out, offering him the swim (just like today, eh?)

It was Len who first went over to using just one single hook. What was happening, we were losing one or two rigs on the wall of the culvert, also sometimes the lead would catch in the cracks running up from the ledge. It was bad news especially for the pike, so Len encouraged us to use a large barbless single hook. Then if you were unlucky to crack off not too much damage was done. One day it was highlighted, when Len, me, Peter Mann and one of his group were fishing the centre. The morning feeding spell did not materialise, so after a couple of hours Len and I decided to make a move

Hooking in the Avons I lift 26lbs 4 ozs. Yes, yes.

right down the far end of the north side, to one of the corners where I'd had a result the week previous, landing a twenty and two doubles.

After the long walk and our rods cast out, we settled down against the wall looking back towards the centre. Another hour passed by with no action, "I wonder how Pete's doing", I said to Len. "About as good as us, I should

Jeff sets a good fighting curve.

think" he replies. Just then I noticed a lot of activity on the skyline at the centre, you could just make them out, up and down the wall like yo-yo's.

"See that Len they might have a fish" I say, pointing towards the middle, "Yeah it looks like it" Len replied. Five minutes later one of them was running along the wall, "What's he doing now Len?" I ask. Len, peering through his hands, "Looks like he's jumping up and down waving his arms, I think he's trying to draw our attention". "We better get down there", I reply. Len agrees as we hurriedly grab our gear together, and head back down to the centre. As we reach the breakwater, Pete meets us halfway, his hair's sticking out all over the place, his arms are going thirteen to the dozen, he looks quite flustered. "What on earth's the matter Pete", I say. "We've got over 40lbs of pike in the sack" he cries. Len and I look at each other, our mouths nearly hitting the floor. "Who had it Pete, was it you?" I ask. "No unfortunately" he says. "Give us a hand with the weighing lads" says Pete. Len and I lay out the weigh net, scales and unhooking gear. Meanwhile, Peter and his mate are struggling up the steps with the sack, the bulge in it looks huge. We stand there with baited breath as Pete tips out the fish, not one but two. "You prat Peter", I shout. Pete and his mate are rolling about laughing; there, laying before us, not a big forty, but two nice twenties. "I didn't say there was a forty in the sack, I said there was over 40lbs of pike", says Peter giggling. "You should have been here, what a state we were in. My mate gets a run in the south half, strikes and starts to play the fish in. I position the net as a good fish boils near the bank, and as I go to net it another fish boils ten yards out. He was hooked up to two fish, after a lot of fun and games I finally get both fish into the net. When we eventually sort it out, we find the two fish tethered together had run through my mates line". We weighed the two pike, one going 24lbs plus, the other 22lbs. Two lucky pike swam off strongly. It just goes to show how important it is not to break off leaving baited rigs in the water! As we gained experience, we learned where not to put a bait, and when to wind up fast, looking after the pike's welfare.

Some funny blokes turned up that first year, even funnier ones the second with Cat Weasel and Hedgehog (only joking lads)! There were the brothers grim, no matter what subject they discussed, it was grim. Also there was a little chubby bloke who used to walk around the reservoir spinning. When he reached the centre, he would pass the time of day with us. I don't think he ever caught anything. Then as regular as clockwork would say, "Oh dear, I've left my fags in the car" and cadge one of Lens. This went on for weeks.

Len used to smoke Senior Service, I used to roll my own "That blokes getting to me" says Len. "I'll sort him out next time he comes down", I reply. The following week our 'chubby spinner' is on his way down "Here comes the man with no fags Bill" said Len, "Yeah, I see him" I replied. Our friend plonks himself down on top of the wall, I sat down beside him.

"How's it going?" he inquires. "No good, we've not had a fish for weeks", I lie. "I reckon it's all to do with the weather", going through his pockets. "Oh no, I seem to have left my cigarettes in the car". He turns to Len, "Give us a fag" he demands. Moving right up tight to him, I put my hand on his thigh, my nose almost touching his. I look into his eyes, pucker my lips, and say, "Give us a kiss and you can have one". I've never seen anyone move so fast, on his feet and away down the reservoir, never to be seen again! Laughing, Len asks, "What would you have done Bill, if he had called your bluff?". Enough of this. Lets get back to the fishing! As my first season on the 'Big Pond' came to an end, my Mk 4's were in a terrible state. I actually lost the top of one, when my lead got stuck in a crack. Waving the rod about the top joint came off, and disappeared down the line to the lead, and when the line parted so did I with half my rod.

What with the continued casting with big baits, the rods were inadequate. So in the close season I purchased two ten foot compound taper glass blanks, with a test curve of 21/2lbs. I made up the handles with 30ins of cork, and couldn't wait for the coming of the new season to test them. Starting my second season on the reservoir some of the old faces were missing, and new ones had taken their place, most of them coming from the Home Counties Specimen Group. Pat Hart, George Lee, Pete Olley and Bill Bristow, who had a mountain of gear. He had the biggest livebait bucket I'd ever seen, how he carried it all down to the centre I'll never know. Then there was Cat Weasel creeping about on the outside and later on Hedgehog.

Jeff acquired his nickname because he reminded me of John Pertwee as the scarecrow in Cat Weasel, but Colin disputes his nickname of hedgehog. I thought it came about when we were having a discussion on blewets, a mushroom-like fungus that Len used to collect around the reservoir for his tea, and what one could eat or not. We decided that Colin, because he looked like he had a bit of gypsy in him, was partial to hedgehog baked in clay. Anyway, my second season on the Big Pond was going quite well, I'd christened my new rods early with a couple of twenties, and was very pleased the way the rods dealt with the fish, the compound taper bending right through to the handle in the fight.

The centre was still the place to be, although one or two other areas started to throw up a fish or two. There was no.8, a swim about 50 yards from the culvert, so called because no.8 was painted on the wall. Why that crack should produce fish more than any other, I don't know. There was no known

Jeff Ducker (Catweasel) with a 'Big Pond' 20 pounder.

Yet another 20 pounder from the King george Reservoir for Colin Benbrook (Hedgehog) - what a beast and the pike looks mean too!

feature there, the bottom was just like the rest of the reservoir, but obviously there was something out there the pike did like.

It was noticeable that the culvert had its resident pike, with new fish moving in from time to time. Also the fish seemed to run from right to left along the ledge. When the resident pike were not at home in the culvert, with half a dozen anglers fishing two rods, spread over 100 yards nine times out of ten it would be the last rod on the right that would go. So it paid to make sure that rod was yours.

It was in my second season I had my first taste of the algae problem. It was almost fluorescent, used to gradually build up on your line and within an hour it looked like you were fishing with rope. When the algae was in the water, sport became non-existent, it used to hang about for weeks. I can't ever remember a fish coming out when the algae was really bad. There was even one period when the algae was in the reservoir for 2½ months. The reservoir used to fish best from September to mid-November then, as the temperature dropped the fishing became harder in early December, slowing right down, with blanks being the norm.

Fishing two to three times a week most days I'd be the only one there, as some of the regulars gave up. In the run up to Christmas, I'd only had one fish of 11lbs 10ozs, my last twenty weighing 23½ lbs coming out on the 19th November at the pumps. Christmas Eve found me again heading for the centre. A slight mist hung over the reservoir as I put my gear down. Standing on top of the wall I decided to fish one rod in the south half, and one in the north. The mist became a little thicker, with hardly any wind. Making up my first rod, as a slow sinker I hooked up a small bream injected it with air and cast out into the south half. On the second rod was a roach ledgered out into the north end. Sitting on top of the wall, I watched both rods at the same time. I took out a small bottle of the hard stuff and had a swig (well it was Christmas Eve!) Looking down the reservoir I checked to see if any of the lads were coming, but the mist was restricting my view. Out of the corner of my eye I saw the silver paper was off the rod rest in the north half; grabbing the net I was down the steps to the rod. The line was pouring out Putting the pick-up in I struck into a good fish, and after a while a nice twenty goes over the net. I'm over the moon, its a month since my last good fish, I carried her up onto the wall and laid her on the grass. Quickly unhooked she weighed 22lbs 8ozs. Sacking her up, I rebait with a big bleak, a quick squirt of air, and back into the culvert. I settle back down on top of the wall and take a celebratory swig from my bottle.

Removing a 26 pounder from a big hessian sack.

An hour passed with no further action, the mist lifted then came back down again. None of the lads turned up, I suppose it was last minute Christmas shopping? I decided to release the fish, having been in the sack too long. Climbing back on the wall thinking of calling it a day, I checked the rod in the south half. It was away! Pulling into the fish the rod took on a lovely curve, the line was singing. The fish kited to the left but 5 minutes of pressure and she's in the net. Lifting her up onto the wall she feels heavy, checking the dial on the Avons and its in the red, 26lbs 2ozs. Laying her out on the grass, I took a couple of snaps. Wrapping the sack around her I carefully climb back down off the wall. Holding the fish in the water 'til she gained her strength, she slowly disappeared. Back up on the wall the bottle's out again, and I start to do silly walks up and down the bank. As the mist cleared, I noticed somebody fishing in the corner of the north side but I didn't recognise him. He's standing up and looking my way, Christ I hope he hasn't seen me with the fish. Recasting I sat down on the steps trying to keep a low profile. Ten minutes later the north rod is away again, I slowly walk to the rod, so not to draw attention to myself. Picking up the rod I glance to the side, the angler's not there, I strike. Again, I'm met with heavy resistance, after a good fight my third twenty goes over the net. Up on the bank she goes 22lbs 6ozs, I carry her down to the water letting her slip away. Back up on the wall I notice the angler's in the corner again, he must have gone through the gap in the wall. I'm quite high now as I cast out another bait, not with drink, I hasten to add, but with the capture of my last three fish. I've hardly got my breath back, when the line's hissing off the reel on the north rod! My legs don't seem to belong to me anymore, as I float down off the wall to the rod. Setting the hook, I give no line at all as I pump the fish hard to the net. As I unfold the mesh the hook fell out. "Blimey it could be another twenty" I think. I hook in the weigh net, the dial settles 19½ lbs. Returning the fish I didn't bother to re-cast the rod, my gear was all over the place. As I start to tidy up, I notice our friend in the corner walking towards me. "Any luck" he asks, "Alright" I mumble, trying to ignore him. A couple of minutes pass in stony silence as I stare out into the reservoir. Finally, I ask "Had any runs up in the corner mate?" "Yes two, I missed the first one then had a 10½ pounder" he replies. "That's good mate", I say. "I was hoping Len would be up today", said our friend. "You know Len", I ask. "Yes I've known Len for years" he introduces himself, "Tony Pithers". "Bill Palmer", I reply. I thought he was an intruder, but being a friend of Len's he knows the score. As we chat, I can't hold out any longer, blurting out my successes. "Yes, I know you had some good fish", says Tony. I baited up the rod that was against the wall, and cast it out, "Come on Tony bring your gear down here, the centre's fishing its head off, there's plenty of room". "No I reckon you cleared them out Bill", replies Tony, as he starts to head back to the corner. He'd walked about 20 yards, when the rod I'd just cast out was away. "Tony", I shout as I strike into the fish. Tony returns, standing up on the wall he starts to give a running commentary. The fish feels like another good one as it runs off to the right. I try to turn it, but have to backwind with the power of the fish. "How's it feel Bill, is it a big one?" Tony inquires. "I don't know, it don't feel bad", I say feeling under complete control. I have the fish close to the bank now, just under the surface when again it makes a screeching run to the right. On seeing the fish, Tony whispers, "I don't want to scare you

Worms eye view of a brace.

Bill, but whatever you do don't lose this one". I nearly have a heart attack, I've just landed 3 twenties, up to 26lbs 2ozs plus a 19½ pounder, and Tony makes a comment like that. I go to pieces, it's an age before I'm back in charge and Tony lands the fish. It wasn't a monster but still a very big fish going 24lbs 8ozs. Tony takes a photo or two and we return her. As I sit on the wall, my head racing, the pictures of the fish coming and going in my mind. I know I've had a drink but I wasn't having hallucinations, I've just made a pike catch of a lifetime, four 20 pounders and a 19½ lbs fish in the same day.

The rest of the season's an anti-climax for me, with just two more doubles falling to my rods. I believe one or two more twenties fell to my mates, but overall it became very hard. We tried tying some herrings on light line, casting them out around the left hand corner on the north side, breaking off the line at the rod, and tying on a small stake pressing it in one of the cracks. We checked the baits all that week, but they lay untouched. We then tried leap frogging around the reservoir but with little success. So ends my second season on the 'Big Pond'.

Looking at the records of my third season on the reservoir, it seemed we didn't normally start fishing there 'til September. But this next year we were there on the 15th June, doing a night for tench. In the close season of that year we spotted some big fish rolling when we were having a walk round, so we started a baiting up programme taking it in turns to put in half a dozen loaves. It felt strange sitting up there on a warm June night, casting out flake. During the night some big tench rolled over our baits, but apart from line bites and half hearted takes we blanked. Dawn came and went, 7 o'clock we were still fishless. Looking in my rucksack, I just happened to have a small pack of deadbaits with me. I made up a pike rod and injected a 6" roach with air, casting it out in the south half. (I don't think Len approved). Placing the rod on the rests I asked Jeff to keep an eye on it as I went down the bank to relieve myself. Returning, Jeff's into a fish, the roach was taken as I disappeared. The pike went 20lbs 12ozs. Going back to the tench, I don't think there was a large head of them, but the few I saw were lumps.

It was also that year I saw the chub. The sun was already up as I walked along on top of the wall, and I spotted seven fish swimming about 10 yards out and a foot under the surface. At first I thought they were small common carp, but putting on my Polaroids and with the sun behind me on closer inspection they turn out to be chub, and bloody big ones. The smallest I estimated at 5lbs, the biggest I'm not going to tell, you would only laugh. When I told the lads, Len said "there was a rumour a few years back of a big chub caught on a spinner weighing 8lbs".

After my encounter with the chub, on all my future pike trips I carried a few bits and pieces just in case I made contact again. Although I was always looking out for them, on my last years on the 'Big Pond' I never did spot them again. I suppose that's the ultimate in hard angling, trying to catch so few fish in so much water. That third season my son, Bernard joined me on most of my trips to the reservoir, fishing the Lea he kept us all in livebaits. I think it was that year Len came out with his plastic indicator flags. It was so simple, but brilliant. When I first fished the 'Big Pond' I used washing up tops for indicators, but when there was a strong wind the undertow made them useless. We then started to use strips of silver paper trapping the line around the back rod rest. The only trouble with this method, every so often the silver paper would run up to the first eye jamming itself. So Len came up with a plastic strip rapped around the rod rest and held together with an elastic band. You put the rod on the rests pulled the flag up the rod rest to just under the reel; open the pickup taking the line to the flag trapping it between the two ends of the plastic. You could reduce or increase the tension on the line by moving the elastic band forwards or backwards.

Painting them fluorescent you could see them 100 yards away, running your eye along a string of rods you would instantly see when a flag was down! When a pike pulled the line out of the plastic, it slid down the rod rest, and we would often hear the flag hit the stone bank. As I said, they were brilliant when used with a running lead, but not to be used with freelined or paternoster rigs. I still carry a couple in my bag to this day, using them right up to the '80's. That season we moved a lot more around the reservoir trying to find new holding areas. But apart from the two corners on the right-hand side of the north half, and the bank in between, it was hard going.

In the south half I had two fish in the left-hand corner by the car park, and

Len and Colin waiting for a run. Notice the flags on the back rod rests.

one of the smallest pike I caught on the reservoir, going 7½ lbs at the towers. I believe Len and Terry had a good period on the front wall in the south half two years earlier, landing a number of fish in a weeks fishing, three of them topping twenty pounds. My third season on the reservoir ended with a personal total of six twenties, keeping up my average of the last two years, landing six and seven twenties respectively. When the fishing became really hard on the 'Big Pond', we did fish other waters, landing some good fish from the valley and another of the London reservoirs. But just like a gigantic magnet the 'George' kept drawing us back.

My fourth year on the 'Big Pond' saw most of us now using just a large single hook for all our fishing on the reservoir. We found a Mustad hollow point 4826 1/0 a very good hook. Pete Olley was a salesman at the time, and on his travels brought up all the stock he could find. Sharing it out between five of us they lasted me out for 25 years. Using mainly bleak the big single hook was ideal; a bleak about 6 to 7 inches long air injected was one of the

Playing a big fish off the broken concrete swim with the gang in attendance.

most successful baits on the reservoir. It was also a very good bait for me on some of the other waters I fished. It was underrated and hardly ever used. On the odd occasion when I fished a bigger bait I reverted back to a couple of no.6 trebles. Len stuck to his guns even when we were using mackerel. He would cut a 1" cutlet out of the middle of a mackerel nicking the big single into the cutlet. He had his fair share of fish on it too. That's how it became known as the "John West" or "middle cut" rig. He took it a stage further by mincing up the bait, placing it in a muslin bag then tying it up with an elastic band. As Colin said, this became the "old plum duff" rig. I don't think Len caught any fish on it, but he swears he did have a run, and missed it.

Only five of us were fishing hard on the reservoir by then, Len, Jeff, Colin, Pete and me. The amount of time we were spending there, I reckon if we took a brick each with us on every trip, we could have built a house.

Talking of bricks, one day Len was pacing up and down measuring the distance between two gaps. "What you doing Len?" I ask. "Counting the bricks" he replies. "Counting the bricks, what you counting bricks for?", I question. "I'm calculating how many bricks there are around the reservoir", said Len. Blimey, there must be millions of them, the things we got up to when the fishing was slow!

That reminds me about getting up to things. There used to be a post in the middle of the centre, it was there to hold a lifebuoy, which had been missing for years. On this particular day I was sitting at the centre, having not had a run for weeks. I climbed up on the post, looking out over the reservoir and I shouted, "Give us a sign, give us a sign". Out of the corner of my eye I saw one of my indicators drop to the ground, I was down off the post in seconds. The resulting run gave me a nice upper double. After that we often climbed the post. Anyone walking around the reservoir, on seeing somebody sitting on top of a post in the middle of the reservoir, shouting out, "Give us a sign", probably thought we were completely mad.

It was in December of that year with a bitter cold north-easterly wind blowing, Bernard had made his way up the reservoir from the Lea where he had been fishing. Sitting on the banks of the Lea, he was exposed to the full force of the wind, he looked blue. With teeth chattering and two dew drops hanging, "Dad, take us home please I'm freezing", he cries. Now for Bernard to want to go home it must have been cold. He was keener than me when I was a boy and that's saying something. "Okay son, I'll just get my gear together", I say taking pity on him. It's 1.30 as I start to pack away on top of the wall, when I see a big fish boil just off the broken concrete in the south half. "God that's a lump", I think to myself, not telling the lads who are fishing the north half. "I'm just dropping Bernard home, I'll be back in a couple of hours", I say leaving my gear on the bank.

I work it out with a bit of luck I'll have about 1 hours fishing left, time I walk back to the car, the journey home, then back again. It's gone three, when I arrive back at the centre. "How's Bernard?", Len inquires. "He's alright now, tucked up in front of the fire with a hot drink", I reply. "Had any runs since I've been gone Len?", I ask. "No you haven't missed anything", said Len. Taking one of my rods, I put on a large roach as a slow sinker and make my way to the broken concrete. Dropping it 40 yards out I let it slowly sink to the bottom, after a couple of minutes I give it a twitch, then let it settle again. I'm gradually working the bait back when the pike takes. Striking into the fish the rod takes on a lovely curve as I have to give line. The lads are up and over the wall giving me encouragement; two minutes later Jeff slips the net under the fish. Up on the bank she's safely unhooked and weighed, going 25lbs 10ozs. She looked a young fish and one we didn't recognise. Taking measurements she's just 40" long, most of the mid-twenties we'd had to date being well over 40". Looking back now the big twenties we caught were probably old fish and past their prime, being very big fish at one time. Apart from Peter Mann's 30lb fish, and Ray Taylor's 28½ lbs caught that first year on the reservoir, no other fish have come through to match them.

With the capture of the new young fish we reckoned the future looked a bit brighter. Towards the end of that season on the 'Big Pond', a new face appeared on the scene, Tony Strover. Although mainly a carp angler Tony was to become a good friend over the next two years. Teaming up with Tony his enthusiasm for the carp rubbed off on me, and I would accompany him on some of his trips, visiting my old haunts in Kent. Fishing particles before they had become widely used we took the waters apart. I would fish the 'Big Pond in the morning, then Tony would have me fishing Dartford for the carp that evening. On one or two occasions, we came close to landing a twenty pound carp and pike on the same day.

Back on the Big Pond, the perch were trying to make a comeback, but unfortunately not too successfully. 3-4 inch fish turned up dead still covered in sores. Remembering my first year fishing the reservoir, on unhooking a fish it would cough up a load of sticklebacks, they seemed to congregate in the culvert in their thousands and were full of tape worms. They were gross, all swollen up looking like miniature mirror carp. "Blimey, the pike can't survive on a diet of diseased sticklebacks," I thought. It was in the early years, one day we were discussing on what the pike might be feeding. I said, "They possibly could be taking the gulls off the top, or eating the dead ones that hit the cables when coming in to roost for the night". There must have been tens of thousands of them paddling about as the light begins to go. I can just imagine a big old pike slowly drifting up to the surface plucking one off the top, then sinking back down again. A couple of months later a known big fish "one gill" was caught, and as she's unhooked the lads discover a pair of feet sticking out from her throat, belonging to a Herring Gull!

When walking around the reservoir we would check the corner the wind was blowing into. The surface would be covered in gull feathers, with the odd dead one, now and again we would find a big old roach that had passed away.

Some of the roach must have gone well over 3lbs. Wasn't it Peter Butler, and the London Specimen Group that had fished for them in the sixties? Checking the corners one day, I noticed dozens of contraceptives floating about. In the weeks that followed they gradually built up 'til there were hundreds of them and I started to wonder how they have arrived in the reservoir, thinking somebody must have been enjoying themselves! I was getting quite concerned about the water quality and where the waterboard was drawing it from. We finally worked it out, the gulls were the likely culprits feeding on sewage farms probably mistook the contraceptives as fish intestines, swallowing then regurgitating them as they roost on the reservoir at night.

After a days fishing on the 'Big Pond', I'd shout down to Bernard who was on the Lea to pack up and to meet me on top of the reservoir bank, we would then make our way down to the car park. One evening walking back to the car, Bernard was lagging behind. "Come on Bernard move yourself", I tell him. He was keeping about 25 yards behind me and in the half-light I caught him bending down from time to time picking something up. "What you found then?", I ask as we arrive back at the car. "Nothing", Bernard replied. "Don't tell me porkies, what you got in your pockets?", I demand. "Nothing", he replied again. "Lets have a look then", I say. He put his hands in his pockets and pulled out two handfuls of bloody big beetles, his pockets were full of them. They were stag or dung beetles, bloody horrible things. The next couple of months, I made sure Bernard emptied his pockets before letting him into the car.

My last season on the 'Big Pond', we started to fish there in late summer, the weed still reaching to the surface around the margins.

Tony and I arrived late one afternoon, it had been hot all day I was keen to try out my new fish finder! We made our way to the right-hand corner where the weed was thickest. "What do you reckon Bill, shall we make a start here?", asked Tony. "Yeah, this looks as good a place as any", I say, making up a slow sinker. My fish finder starts to undress, putting on a snorkel, goggles and flippers he quietly slips into the water. "Where to?" Tony asks. "Right along the weed bed", I say. Tony starts to swim along the first weed bed hardly making a ripple, swimming on the surface looking down into the water. Suddenly Tony's arm is in the air, bending at the elbow he points down into the water. Letting him move 20 yards further on, I drop the roach into the spot where he had pointed to. I fed the line out as the bait slowly sinks to the bottom; the line stops. Holding the rod up high, so the line didn't sink into the weed bed, I trapped the line between my fingers. My eyes went back to Tony, searching the second weed bed. I feel a slight tensioning of the line, then its pulled free. "Tony we're away", I shout. Striking into the fish, it goes absolutely crazy in the warm water. I finally hand it out covered in weed and weighing about 12lbs; my fish finder works, me thinks!

Ten minutes later Tony is pointing again, nodding his head he looks quite excited. I let him swim clear before casting another roach into the area, tight to the second weed bed.

My fish finder makes his way to the bank, thirty yards further down the reservoir, as my face registers a run. The line was leaving the reel at an alarming rate of knots, then started to slow, I put in the pick up, letting the fish pull the line tight to the rod.

I sweep the rod back, nothing. "Dam", or words to that effect, I say, as Tony comes along beside me. "You missed it Bill", my fish finder asks. "Yeah, it was a screaming take", I reply. "Shame, it was a lump well over twenty pounds", said Tony as he dried himself off. "Oh well, you win some you lose some, there's always another day. But there wasn't, the weather made a change for the worse, becoming very cold. Trying my hardest, I could not coax my fish finder back into the water, it seems he just didn't work in cold conditions.

It was before turning cold, about two weeks prior to Tony doing his fish finder act, we had a competition to see if I could play Tony in on my pike tackle. Tying my 10lb line to his shorts, I let him have 30 yards of line before starting to fight. Being a good swimmer Tony's out into the middle of the culvert in seconds. "Right go, Tony", I shout. Tony dives straight down, my 10ft, 2½ lbs t.c. rod went over bending right through to the very end of the handle, before the clutch started to sing. I played him off the clutch, normally I'd backwind, but seeing it's only a bit of fun, I had set the clutch to the limit of my line. Within ten minutes, Tony was exhausted and played out. As I beached him one of the lads asks for a gaff saying, "I'll lift him out for you Bill".

Anyway, back to the real fishing. Bernard was coming up to thirteen now and I let him fish with me on the reservoir from time to time. I believe the rules on juniors stated they had to be fourteen and accompanied by an adult, Bernard being quite a big lad would pass for fourteen.

Late January found Bernard and I fishing the reservoir on our own, apart from a fish just scraping doubles, it was slow. It was well into the afternoon when I had a run in the culvert in the north half. Slamming into the fish, I knew right away it was a good one. Fighting well the fish comes to the net three times, only to bore off into the middle of the culvert again. When the fish came in the fourth time, I could see she was a lump. Bernard was shaking, but he slipped the net under her with no bother. "Did the size of the fish scare you", I asked. "No, I was afraid you would thump me if I messed up the netting and lost the fish", he replied. I love him really. The fish, a beauty carrying a bit of spawn, weighed 26lbs 12ozs.

As the season drew to a close, I was to land my biggest fish on the 'Big Pond', 'one gill', going 27lbs 4ozs, I believe at her heaviest weight. My life was about to change with a new job at Fords, and a new bungalow at Pitsea. So, regrettably my time on the 'Big Pond' came to an end.

Summing up, fishing on the King George reservoir, I entered the big time catching fish I only dreamed about before. I believe we probably just missed out on some truly big fish by a couple of years. If only we had been on the water when the perch swam in their thousands, who knows what we might have landed? The tagging certainly opened my eyes showing how quickly a few decent anglers can catch most of the fish, even on very big waters. In five short years, we saw well over 100 twenties caught, my personal tally being about 30. Len, Jeff and Colin, fished on for another five years or so taking a

One gill weighing 27¹/⁴ pounds.

A young Bernard posing with one gill.

lot more fish, up to just under 28lbs. The water was in very good hands.

I loved the freedom there, being able to fish how I wanted, to use what bait I chose, put out another rod without looking over my shoulder, fishing with good friends. Being responsible anglers, we did not abuse our freedom as the fishing proved.

Most pike waters last a couple of years, if they are lucky. Looking after our fish, on the 'Big Pond', it fished well for ten years, and more.

I did return a few times, 20 years later, the first time with Bernard and Wayne Sutton. On arriving at the centre there was an angler crouching down by the wall, fishing 6 rods spread over about 50 yards, two of them either side of the culvert on the north side. "How's it going?", I ask. "Grunt", he replies. "Oh, as good as that", I say. "Grunt", he replied again. "How about moving a couple of rods, and give my mate a chance", I say. All I got was another grunt. I said, "What about moving a couple of rods, be fair". With that it finally spoke, as he starts to gather all his rods together, "It's obvious you haven't fished here before, it's not that good", he tells me. "It was, twenty odd years ago", I replied laughing. He scurried away looking like a giant porcupine, with rods sticking out from all over him. The last time, I went back was in 1993, with Steve Wells, my present fishing partner, trying to catch him a twenty from my old haunt. Carp were jumping out all over the place though we did have fish. I had a 14lb pike, Steve landing an 18½ pounder on a paternostered perch. With the bivvies mushrooming up, perhaps in time the reservoir will do some massive carp in the future. But for me, I'll always remember it as the 'Big Pond', a bloody good pike water.

SMALL AIR INJECTED DEAD BAIT RIG 1

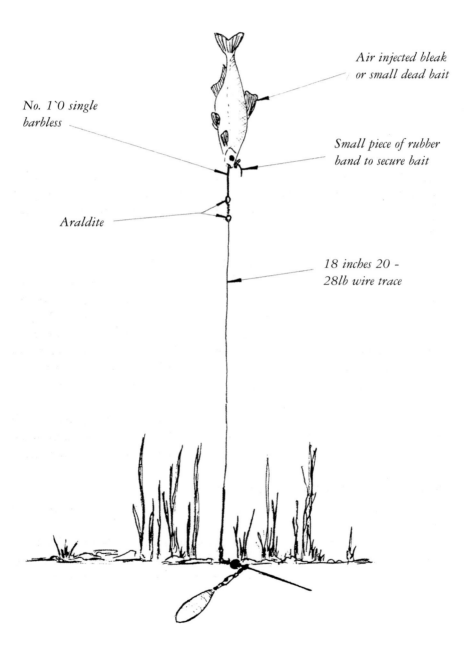

Air injected bleak
or small dead bait

No. 1`0 single
barbless

Small piece of rubber
band to secure bait

Araldite

18 inches 20 -
28lb wire trace

3

RIGS

Not wanting to teach anyone how to suck eggs, I'd like to mention just a few rigs that have been successful for me over the last 25 years. Many of them originated from my days at the King George Reservoir.

RIG 1: SMALL AIR INJECTED DEADBAIT RIG

This was the first air injected rig we used on the 'Big Pond' to beat the silkweed problem, using mainly bleak for bait it caught us a lot of fish. So simple but very effective with the big barbless single there is no hooking or unhooking problem, a brilliant rig with small baits. Using a hypodermic syringe, put the needle just under the bait's scales and squirt a small amount of air into the fish. The bait pops straight up off the bottom. Bleak were made for this rig, not growing more than 6-8 inches and weighing about 1 ounce, they are perfect.

This rig has certainly caught more than a few fish over the years, though why the bleak are so successful, I don't know. Perhaps its something to do with the fishes scales, which were used in the production of artificial pearls.

RIG 2: SMALL POLY'D LIVEBAIT RIG

If my life depended on me catching pike this is the rig I would use - one of my all-time favourites.

Again, a very simple rig, basically the same as Rig 1, the only difference being the small piece of polystyrene wired to the eye of the hook. I normally carry with me about 20-30 different sizes of polystyrene wired up ready to use. To make up it will cost you nothing, all you need is some high density polystyrene, which you can pick up anywhere; nearly everything is packed in it now. Take a small piece of plastic coated electric wire, cut into 5 inch lengths and strip off the plastic coating leaving about 20 strands of thin copper wire. Cut the polystyrene into different sizes with a sharp knife, I cut mine into barrel shapes. Put one of the strands of copper wire into the eye of a large sewing needle and pass it through the middle of the polystyrene. Twist the wire together securing your poly leaving about 2 inches of wire to fit to the hook. Select the piece of poly suited to the size of bait you are going to use. Wire it on to the eye of the hook, and cast out.

RIG 3: POLYLIVE TWO TREBLE RIG

With bigger baits I use two no.6 trebles, fixing the poly to the eye of the second hook. You can mount the bait either way round, although I prefer to set the second hook and poly into the root of the tail of the bait. With bigger baits a larger piece of poly is needed.

RIG 4: DEAD-AND-LIVE RIG

As an alternative method to suspend a livebait off the bottom, I started to experiment with small air injected deadbaits and lives, finding it quite a good catching rig. Using a dead bleak or small roach air injected on the first hook I then put a small livebait on the second hook. Gudgeon work well. And I found it a good rig when the pike are fry feeding.

RIG 5: SLOW SINKER RIG

Another rig that's been good to me over the years, catching me some big fish. It came about by accident after I had cast to a fish that had boiled on the surface of the 'Big Pond'. I was fishing an air injected roach of about 8 ounces at the time and had nipped a swan shot on for a stop to the lead. Taking the lead off I had cast to the fish, only for the bait to float on the surface being full of air. Winding in I squeezed out some air and dropped it back in the water. The swanshot upended the bait and it slowly sank into the depths. I cast to the fish, and half way down in 20 odd feet of water the pike took and the slow sinker was born.

It works well in deep clear reservoirs and pits, a good rig to cast to striking fish. I believe the splash of the bait hitting the surface also alerts the pike

SMALL POLYED LIVE ON SINGLE RIG 2

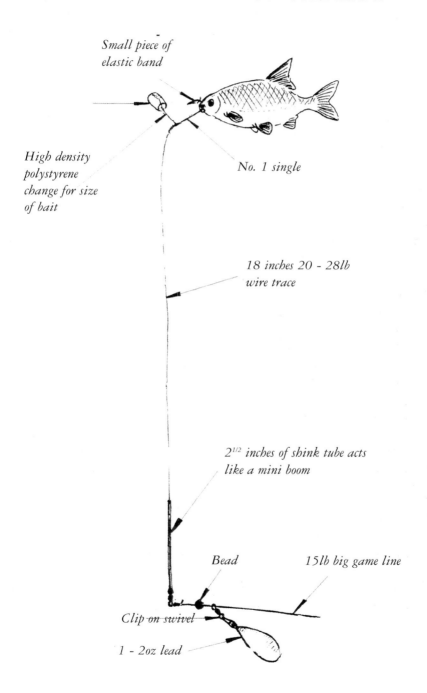

Small piece of
elastic band

High density
polystyrene
change for size
of bait

No. 1 single

18 inches 20 - 28lb
wire trace

2¹ᐟ² inches of shink tube acts
like a mini boom

Bead

15lb big game line

Clip on swivel

1 - 2oz lead

POLY LIVE TWO TREBLE RIG 3

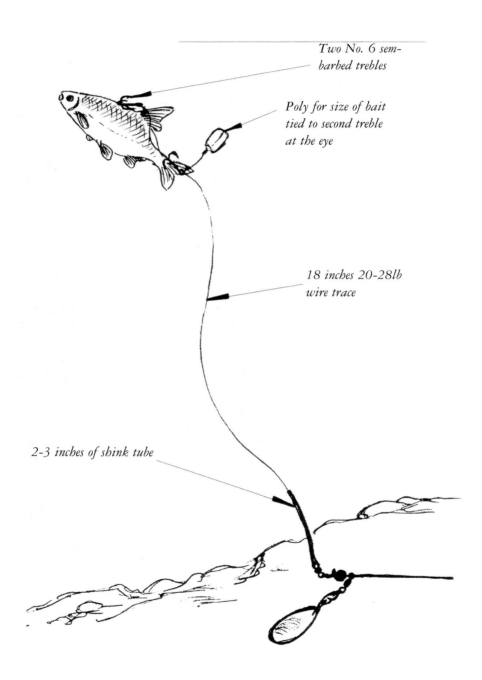

Two No. 6 sem-barbed trebles

Poly for size of bait tied to second treble at the eye

18 inches 20-28lb wire trace

2-3 inches of shink tube

drawing its attention to the bait as it sinks very slowly down to the bottom.

A minute or two after the bait hits bottom lift the rod and wind in a yard of line repeating every couple of minutes. Natural baits work best, roach, rudd, chub, dace and bream between 2-12 ounces.

With the bait injected with air, put just enough swanshot on to up-end the bait; the slower it sinks the better. Add more air or squeeze some out to finely balance the bait. The rig works well over weed, dropping it down lightly on to the weed, lifting it up then dropping it down again. It's very important, when using the slow sinker not to neglect your rod, always be in contact with the bait at all times. If you don't you might end up with a deep hooked pike. I have found that when pike take the slow sinker, feeling no resistance they will not always run with the bait. It's a good idea therefore to have a clip-on swivel on the line, then if you want to put the rod down, all you have to do is clip on a lead, place the rod in the rests, and turn on the backbiter - you are now fishing a normal deadbait rig.

RIG 6: EEL SECTION AIR INJECTED RIG

Eel is a very good bait for sorting out the better fish. It casts well, and even very small chunks when air injected hold air very well; high in protein the pike love them. The eel must be an easy target for the pike, being half buried with 2-6 inches of head and body sticking up out of the mud - old esox scenting them out, slowly drifting down and snapping them up! It pays you sometimes when fishing a head section to spend a little time in setting up the bait. Add a couple of swanshot to the trace, then put in just enough air to make the bait look like it's poking out of the silt.

I remember a few years back cutting up a big eel for a session on Lakeside. Arriving at the pit I set up and selected the 6 inch head section from the bag. It was still throbbing and twisting in my hand as I tried to put in the hooks.

As I nicked on the second treble the eel arches itself and bites into my hand. I couldn't believe it being over an hour since I had cut up the eel. I had to use forceps to remove the bait from my hand. What an incredible lump of eel it turned out to be, catching me a dozen pike that day. As I packed up and unhooked the bait, after 10 hours fishing, it was still throbbing in my hand. Supposedly, it was just the eel's nerves. Blimey that's some sort of nervous system!

DEAD AND LIVE RIG 4

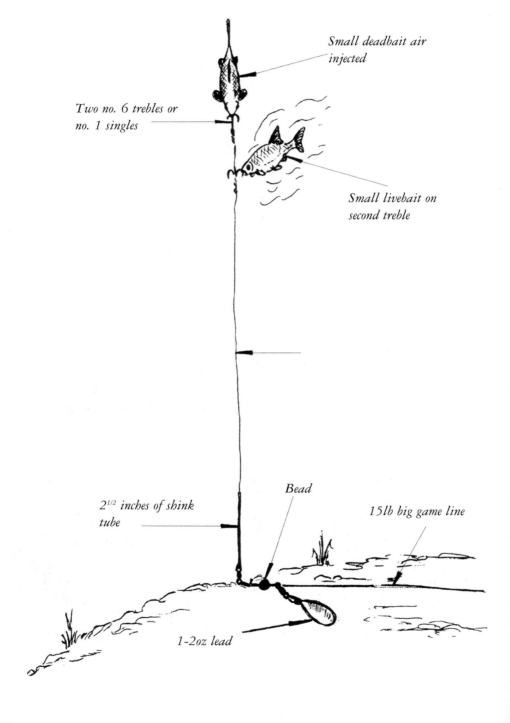

Small deadbait air injected

Two no. 6 trebles or no. 1 singles

Small livebait on second treble

Bead

2¹ᐟ² inches of shink tube

15lb big game line

1-2oz lead

SLOW SINKER RIG 5

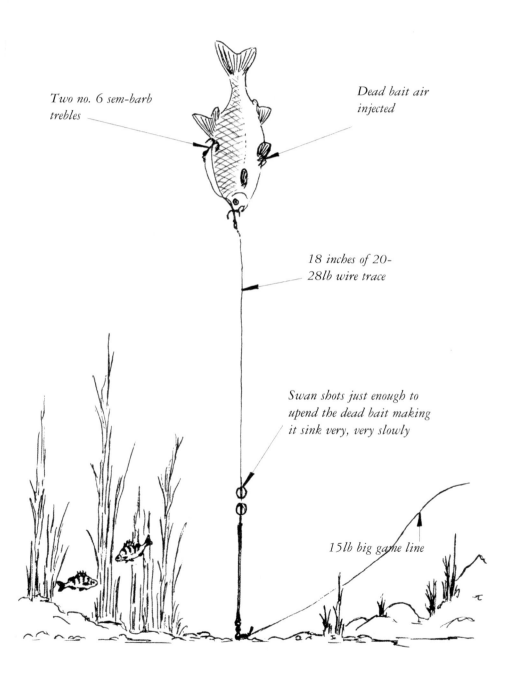

Two no. 6 sem-barb trebles

Dead bait air injected

18 inches of 20-28lb wire trace

Swan shots just enough to upend the dead bait making it sink very, very slowly

15lb big game line

EEL SECTION AIR INJECTED RIG 6

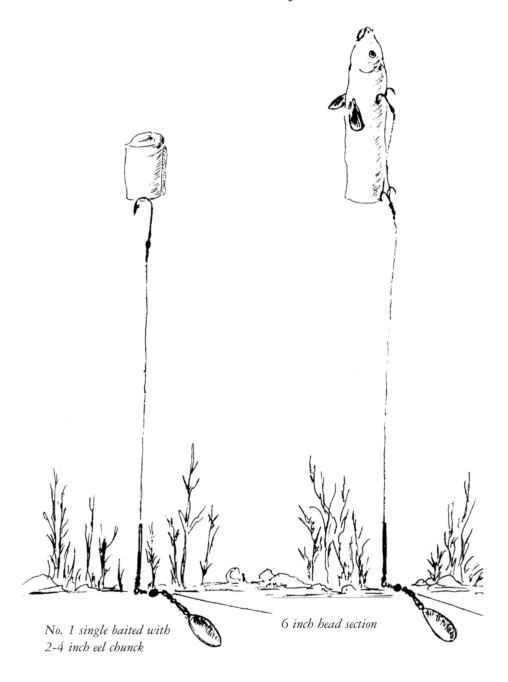

No. 1 single baited with
2-4 inch eel chunck

6 inch head section

4

MONSTERS AND MYTHS

No other fish stirs up the imagination more than the pike. Over the years there has probably been more rubbish spoken about it than any other fish.

In my early pike days, I would always be chasing about checking out rumours of monsters found dead or seen at such-and-such a lake or pit, though never by a pike angler, it was always by a dog walker or non-fisherman. I finally dismissed all these sightings after one day while fishing a large lake in Essex, another angler brought it home to me. Releasing a nice double weighing 15 1/2lbs, I was well pleased with myself as I drank a well deserved cup of tea; a mid-double from a pit is a good fish by anybody's standard. Picking up my free 'rover' rod I was about to re-bait when an angler fishing in a bay 40 yards along the bank came running towards me.

"Oi mate, Oi mate" shouting at me, at the top of his voice. "Blimey", I thought to myself, "what have I done", as I cower behind a tree. "You're pike fishing ain't yer mate?", the angler screeched, "Well, er yes", I answered. "Get yourself down here mate, there's a f****** great f****** pike in my swim, its got to be f****** forty pounder if it's an ounce", he said frothing at the mouth.

"How big?", I said, grabbing a couple of baits from the net, and putting them into a bucket. "Forty pounds, it's a f****** monster", he replied with excitement. With my free rover rod, net and baits I quickly follow him back to his swim. As I arrive in the bay, I catch sight of the pike's back, then tail as it disappears into the depths leaving a trail of bubbles on the surface. "Did yer see it mate, did yer see it, bloody huge ain't it?", my friend said pointing to the spot. Seen it, I'd just unhooked it! Yes it was the 15 1/2lb fish that I had released a couple of minutes ago. It was probably slightly gassed up, and had surfaced in our friends swim, finally expelling the last of the air as I arrived. "You going to cast a bait out then?", our friend asks. "No, it could be anywhere now, I'll wait to see if it comes to the surface again", I say, just checking that the pike's alright.

I hadn't the heart to tell him it wasn't a monster, I don't think he would have believed me anyway. "How long you been fishing" I ask him. "Ten years mate", he replied. "Have you ever seen a pike as big as that before?", I inquired. "No, I didn't think there was monster pike as big as that in here, wait 'til I tell my mates what I've seen", he said.

I believe we've all been guilty to some degree of exaggerating in our angling lives, through being inexperienced, or over-excited seeing a large fish on the surface we over-estimate it, just like our friend. Then there's the time when we hook into a fish, after a minute or two with the rod well over the line breaks or the hook pulls out. "Blimey, that was a big fish". We've all said it haven't we, only for it to be caught sometime later and it turns out to be no monster. There's the pike or carp that fights like hell, all over the place you just cannot control it, but after a long, exhausting fight its finally landed. You discover the fish is foul hooked in the flank or tail, and is not as big as you imagined. If you hook a fish in very shallow water, it explodes into action, the line's a blur as its stripped from the reel. As the fish bow waves across the lake, if you lose the fish it becomes a monster. So knowing all this, when an angler talks about monsters I take it with a pinch of salt, until that is, one day while fishing a Lea valley pit it happened to me.

At the time I was still on the 'Big Pond', though Jeff Ducker had fished the water in the past with his brother-in-law, Roland. Owls pit it was called.

I'd fished most of the Lea valley pits, but up to now this one had eluded me. I'd been told the stories about the monster pike, lost in a sunken orchard by Roger Smith, Jack Hilton, and others, also a massive fish lost at the net.

But being on a half decent water myself, I wasn't that interested at the time, to tear down there to fish it. In the 1973 season the 'Big Pond' was going through a dour period so Jeff persuaded me to have my first trip to Owls pit. Jeff filled me in on the water, "Mackerel's the bait there, the pike won't touch herrings, they haven't caught for years", he tells me. "Right Jeff", I replied. At the fishmongers buying 1/2 dozen herrings, I reason that if they haven't caught for years, it's about time they did. Jeff, Len and I arrived at the pit at first light, we decided to give the south bank a go. With

Stringways pit behind us we settled down into our swims. Fishing both rods with air injected baits I have fish from the off, four jacks in the first two hours. I believe Len and Jeff had a number of jacks too, so I put on one of the herrings and cast it 50 yards out freelined. As I put on the indicator, I noticed I'm already away. Striking instantly, not waiting at all, I then remembered I'd put on a whole herring! The fish gave a good account of itself, with a lot of head shaking and I finally slipped the net under a good double. On the scales she weighed just under 16lbs. "What you have it on Bill?", Jeff asks. "Herring", I say with a smug look on my face, I don't think Jeff believed me. I finished my first day on the pit, with another jack or two, and a fish of 9lbs.

It wasn't 'til the last week of the season that I returned for my second session on Owls pit. March 9th 1974 found Jeff, Colin, Len and I fishing by the pumps on the 'Big Pond'. We'd been there from first light, giving it our best shot. The centre wasn't fishing, and what with strong cold, north east winds fishing the pumps we had the shelter and protection of the north wall. Midday, and we were fishless, not one of us had a run. "I've had enough of this, lets go down the pub for a pint then fish the last two hours on Owls pit", moans Jeff. I don't think Colin or Len needed their arms twisted and it sounded good to me. With the gear packed away in record time, ten minutes later we were sitting in the warm pub the feeling having come back into our limbs as the cold left our bones. With a nip or two inside me I was quite content to see the day out in the pub but come 2 o'clock we were turfed out into the cold. As we arrive at Owls pit the wind was cutting right through us as we made our way round to the north bank. Some bungalows border that side of the pit, offering us some protection from the bitter cold wind. I picked a swim with bull rushes to my right and a sunken bush to my left. About 80 yards out I could see the tips of branches poking from the water. Len, Colin and Jeff went further along the bank fishing close to the point. Assembling my rods, I put in the rod rests and checked the bait bag - 4 good size bleak and 3 nice roach up to 12ozs.

"Right, there are supposed to be some biggies in here, lets go for it", I think to myself as I pick out the largest roach. I set the bait up as a slow sinker injected some air into the roach and tested it in the water. I had to add another swanshot to the bigger bait, then cast it 40 yards out. Sitting back into my seat I rubbed my hands together trying to get some feeling back into numbed fingers. Twenty minutes pass with no action.

Some life was coming back to my hands, so I decided to put my second rod out dropping a pumped up bleak under the sunken bush in the margins. I'd reached the time in the day when a jack will do, a run, anything to save a blank. Watching my lines where they enter the water, the one with the roach lifted 2 inches, then dropped back. Rubbing my eyes, did that move? It lifted again, the silver paper starting to creep up as I stand over the rod. Letting a couple of yards run off the reel I put in the pickup then wound down to the fish. The line tightened, pulling the rod back it stopped in its tracks only half way up as a heavy weight moved off. "Jeff", I shout, knowing I'm into a good fish. It was heading straight out very slowly, putting more pressure on the fish the rod took on more of a curve as I gave line. I put on as much pressure as I dared but I was still making no impression on it as it headed into the pit. "Jeff, Len, Colin", I shout again, getting quite concerned as the fish nears the branches sticking out of the water. The fish hadn't veered off its course, or altered its speed since I hooked it. Holding the rod up high there was over 60 yards of line out of the water and I was still having to backwind. "Jeff, Len, anybody", I scream as I now started to panic looking down at the reel. Checking the spool, there was nearly 100 yards of line out but, as the rod started to jerk suddenly the line ground to a halt. Everything went solid but I kept the pressure on the fish for five minutes, then gave up, opened the pickup and placed the rod in the rests. I felt drained. I wanted to fetch the lads, but the thing takes five more yards before going solid again, then the line went slack, the fish had gone. I wound in 90 odd yards of line, and threw the rod into the rushes beside me. Slumping back into my chair completely gob smacked, Jeff appeared. He noticed I was in a bit of a state, and asked what had happened. "I've just been broken by something, it's taken nearly 70 yards of line under very heavy pressure. I could do nothing, it kept going slowly until it reached the snags, I don't believe it". "I told you there are some lumps in here Bill", said Jeff, "A lump, this was something else", I replied. "Come on Bill get the rod out again", Jeff tells me as he picked the rod out of the rushes. "You're joking, what's the point?" I say. "We've still got another hour Bill, you never know", Jeff said, trying to console me. "Oh alright then", I replied, checking the line, just to keep Jeff happy.

Removing the last five yards which was slightly frayed, and tying on a new trace, I hooked up the second biggest roach and pumped some air into it. Casting out, the bait dropped in the exact spot where I'd hooked the monster, (what am I writing, I don't believe in monsters). Clipping the line on the back rod rest with silver paper, I then forgot about it. I started to discuss with Jeff what the hell I'd hooked, could I have foul hooked a massive carp, perhaps a catfish? There was no record of any being caught, so I dismissed both possibilities. It was just like tying your line to a cars rear bumper moving off at two miles an hour, you then try to stop it with a pike rod. Whatever it was, I don't believe the thing knew it was hooked. "Bill, you have a run", Jeff cried, frightening the life out of me. Blimey, I'd forgot all about my rods as the line trickled out, the roach had been taken again. Winding down to the fish I put a good bend into the rod. The fish kited to the right, I applied side strain turning it easily, and had the pike in the margins when it tried to go into the sunken bush. Clamping down hard, I stop it dead, the fish surfaces, a dozen turns of the reel handle and Jeff scoops

24³/⁴ pounds a couple of quick photos before I release my 'consolation' prize.

it up in the net. "It's a twenty Bill", said Jeff as he lies it down on the grass. I peep into the net, Jeff's right it looks a mid-twenty to me. As we go to unhook her we notice the hooks had fallen out in the net. I sack her up while

Jeff goes to fetch Len and Colin. As I sit there reflecting on what's happened in the last half hour I should have been elated with my catch, but I could not get excited at all. I've just landed a mid-twenty, in one minute flat but I can't help pondering on what I'd hooked 25 minutes before. Jeff returned with Len and Colin; I lifted the fish out of the water and we weighed her at 24lbs 12ozs.

The lads took a couple of quick photos, then on the edge of the bull rushes I released my consolation prize. Twenty odd years have passed since that day on Owls pit, and I still have no answer for what happened. Had it taken place today, I'd have sworn my mate Steve Wells had stitched me up, with some of his friends. (Steve runs a scuba diving club). Anyway, do I now believe in monsters, certainly not, well 'er perhaps just a little, but I've kept a keen eye on the pit as the years have rolled by, only fishing there on one or two more occasions. It was some years later, after my incident on Owls pit, Eddie Turner and Bill Hancock were to fish the pit. Bill had his first twenty weighing 27½ lbs, a year later Eddie was to catch his first ever thirty from Owls pit, his first of many. I asked Eddie if he knew of any other big fish caught when he fished there. He told me a noddy had a 30½ lbs fish from their swims around about that time but apart from that one he wasn't aware of any others. So to date, there haven't been any reports of monsters being caught from Owls pit.

5

ABBERTON RESERVOIR

My first visit to Abberton was in the early seventies, late summer, I believe. The Lads and I planned to night fish there for the eels before we started our serious pike fishing on the 'Big Pond'. Colin Broadbent picked up Jeff Ducker and his brother-in-law, Roland, meeting Len Savage and me on the banks of the reservoir. Arriving late afternoon we set up on the 'big half' with two other anglers fishing the reservoir by the culvert. As the light started to fade, using lob worms for bait we soon had a couple of eels in the sack.

Roland landed the biggest so far weighing about 3lbs and it was looking good for the night's fishing to come. I notice Colin licking his lips as Roland dropped his fish into the sack, (I believe Colin was going to make eel and hedgehog pie). Then one of the anglers fishing the culvert walked up to us saying, "Come on lads you have to pack up now". "Pack up, we're going to fish for the eels into the night, leaving our gear out we can watch from our cars", we say. "I'm sorry, but the water board don't allow night fishing, you'll have to leave when its dark", he said telling us he was a honorary bailiff for the water. Not wanting to upset anyone on our first trip to the reservoir, we packed up and left.

Some months later, the five of us were back fishing the shallow half for the pike. Jeff's brother-in-law Roland, until then still had not caught a double; fishing mainly on Owls pit using mackerel he was struggling. Jeff had told him the best place to break his duck was Abberton but by midday only a couple of jacks had been landed and Roland was still to get his first run. We decide to retire to the Fox public house for a quick one leaving Roland on the reservoir to catch his double. On returning Roland still hadn't caught a fish, and time was running out for him. This called for a team effort so we tell Roland he can now have all the runs on all of the rods.

As the last hour approached, we had a feeding frenzy of jacks and it became quite comical as we sat behind our rods, shouting encouragement to Roland as he ran from rod to rod, landing jacks one after the other. Finally, on the very last run of the day Roland was to land his double, weighing just 2ozs over ten pounds.

It was almost five years later before I was fated to return, after those early trips to Abberton. I'd now come off the 'Big Pond', moving into my new bungalow at Pitsea, it was October 1976 and I was about to start my new job with Ford's at Dagenham. The car company was about to launch their small car, the Fiesta. Working nights and days, two weeks about, what an eye opener it turned out to be. Some of the strokes the lads pulled were quite unbelievable, blimey, I could write a book about my time there. Perhaps I will when I retire, selling it to a T.V. company as a comedy, "my life on the line" (dream on Bill, dream on). Working in the P.T.A., final assembly plant we were unfortunately dependent on other plants feeding us with components, engines, bodyshells, paint and so on. When there was a dispute, or the lads stopped work anywhere on the estate we were affected and laid off. My first year with Ford's, with three children to bring up, Sheila and I went through some hard times. It was because of a lay off I was destined to meet up with my old school mate, John Meecham again.

I was on nights. Reporting for work, the foreman informed us we were off pay, the body shop was on strike and we would be laid off. Arriving back home and not tired being in bed all day after my last nights work, it was quite mild for January so I decided to have a couple of hours carp fishing at Dartford.

Setting up by the bridge I dropped both baits under the trees in the margins. Throwing in a tin of corn I then settled back into my chair and it was starting to rain as I checked my watch, midnight. As I sat there listening to the rain hitting the brolly my right hand isotope slams against the rod, I struck into thin air "Round things", I shout winding in my line, when the left hand rod tries to launch itself. The fish had pulled the hook home and was taking a lot of line, reaching the Darenth bank before I turned it. Five minutes later I had it under the rod top, only for it to make another long run. Finally she was ready for netting, the only problem was that there was about an inch of liquid mud on the bank where I was standing, and I was slipping all over the place. In fact, I thought at one stage I was going to join it in the water rather than it joining me on land. The carp weighed 20½ lbs, 15 minutes later I had another fish going 17¼ lbs.

By today's standards that catch wouldn't get a mention in the angling press, but in the 1970's a twenty pound carp was a big fish. Gerry Savage put the story out on his fishing programme on Radio Kent and John, on his way home from work had picked it up on his car radio. Hearing that I was now living in Pitsea, and he at Rayleigh only five minutes away, going through the phone book he soon had my new number. It was good to see John again, being almost ten years since we had fished together with the East Ham Angling Club. John and I also had fished the River Kennet and its tributaries for chub and barbel having some good days. Meeting up with John again was just the shot in the arm I needed as my fishing was going through the doledrums. He was bubbling over with enthusiasm, wanting to catch a decent carp and expecting me to catch him one.

It wasn't 'til the start of the new season that I was to take him to Lake Meadows in Billericay, a small Essex park lake. Setting him up opposite the island and catapulting a couple of tins of corn tight against its margins, I fit him up with 6lbs line link ledgered a no.6 hook baited with three grains of corn. I told him to cast as close as he can to the island. With his two baits out, I moved twenty yards along the bank telling John not to neglect his rods or he could lose one. Ten minutes later, John's out of his chair and was strolling towards me. "I hope you have opened your bale arms John", I say, both looking back at his rods. The nearest one started to shake, the rod rest leaning out into the water. John sprinted back to his swim just grabbing his rod as it bounced off the rest. The fish powered off into the middle of the lake, with John hanging on but a few seconds later the hook pulled out. John recast and settled back into his chair - I think it would have taken gelignite to shift him now as he concentrated on his rods!

Two hours later his patience was rewarded with another run, John going on to land a nice mirror weighing 16½ lbs. I believe that day the seed was sown; John spends all his time carp fishing now. Talking to John later that day he told me he had driven over a large reservoir near Colchester earlier in the week and he fancied fishing it. "Near Colchester, it sounds like Abberton John, I fished it about five years ago for eels, it holds some half decent pike too", I tell him. So we arranged a trip to the reservoir for the coming weekend. On the Saturday John and I travel up to London, fishing the Lea for some bleak to use as deadbaits on the reservoir the following morning. It's funny looking back now how I would spend a day fishing for a few dozen fresh bleak, mind you they certainly caught fish. John picked me up Sunday morning and we headed for Abberton. Upon arriving John drove over the road running to the 'small end'. "What do you reckon Bill, looks good don't it?" said John. "Yeah, its not bad John, but you want the road that goes over the 'big half', I tell him. John put the car into reverse and we make our way to the road running over the 'big half'. John pulled up by the culvert, jumped out and through the gate. Leaning on the wall we looked into the culvert that runs under the road. "Blimey, its big Bill!", said John looking out over the reservoir. "There's about 15 miles of bank I believe John, lets make a start in the 'big half'", I replied. John and I had the gear out in double quick time, and pumped up bleak on large singles were cast out, the lines clipped back on the rod rest with a flag. Both of us were fishing left of the culvert and within minutes John's flag dropped to the ground. His spool was emptying of line in record time. Striking into the fish he soon had it near the bank, but the line zig zagging in the water was a sure sign of an eel. John guided the fish over the net, it weighed nearly 3lbs. From then on it was action all the way. We found 70% of the runs we had came from eels averaging about 2½ lbs, the pike we caught were mainly small.

We knew straightaway when an eel picked up the bait, they absolutely screamed off. What a brilliant day we had, nothing huge, just a real fun day's fishing. We couldn't believe our luck with hardly anybody fishing the reservoir around July and August, when we fished there. I really enjoyed those early trips to Abberton with John, going on to many more fun days. The eel fishing was fabulous, who would have thought that a fish dealer could wipe out the entire eel stock within a year or two after putting down his fyke nets. But that's what happened some years later. I wouldn't have believed it possible to desolate such a big water. It's been many years now since I've had an eel from Abberton. Anyway as I said the eel fishing was very good, but the pike were rather on the small side.

If my memory serves me right, that first year's fishing at Abberton with John in 1976, I only had a few small doubles and loads of jacks. Bernard, I believe went right through the year without catching a double, landing lots of jacks each trip though. The jack explosion was probably due to the big pike being culled. I was told the water company was throwing the pike up the bank when emptying the traps although I don't know if there was any truth in it, all those years ago.

So I made contact with Martin Gay, who had first fished Abberton in the winter of 1967. It was a few years later 1971/72 I believe that Martin had a disagreement with the then bailiff and the manager of the water company. After all these years I was still under the impression it was to do with the culling of the pike, but Martin told me his argument with Essex Water was nothing to do with their netting policy. It was just a misunderstanding about a day's fishing at the valve tower, after the water company had stopped anglers fishing there. Martin went on to tell me there were only locals and Essex Water employees (plus a few in the know) fishing Abberton in the 1967/68 season.

The first winter on the reservoir he reckons sport was pretty good with fish up to 23lbs. The following season was much the same with fish to over 20lbs, not that many doubles but again lots of sport, Martin went on to say. 1970/71 was probably the finest season ever in the history of the place. Huge numbers of small fish up to about six inches, roach and bream had gathered not only at the culvert, but also at the valve tower at the Layer Breton end of the reservoir. Sport was quite fantastic at times with lots of doubles and several over 20lbs.

Martin's best ever Abberton fish (27½ lbs) was taken that November but the best hauls of quality fish were made at the valve tower. In three trips during October 1970 he and friends caught 26, 39 and 29 pike for a total weight (if his memory serves him well), of over 900lbs. The following seasons (before he stopped fishing there) were never as prolific, but he did get some good fish up to 26lbs.

Well that's Martin's brief account of his time on Abberton, still leaving me a couple of years I've not been able to fill in, taking us up to the time when I returned with John in 1976. Some of the anglers fishing there when we returned had their very own personal brick, using it to smash the odd pikes head in. The rules at the time I believe allowing you to take two sizeable fish if you so wished. They used to keep the bricks in the storm pipes that run into the reservoir. Many a time when arriving I'd go and check the pipes throwing any bricks I found into the culvert. Thankfully it didn't last long, the anglers finally being persuaded to return all their fish. A few years later when Vic Gibson was fishing the water, if the odd angler looked like he was going to dispatch a fish he would offer him a couple of quid. Telling him if he wanted to eat fish he should buy it at the fish shop.

They soon got the message! As each year passed the pike fishing became better, improving all the time with quite a lot of doubles and a good sprinkling of twenties.

Some years the amount of fry in the culvert was incredible, there must have been millions of them. As it started to get light, like a big black cloud the fry would move out into the reservoir to feed. I noticed if there was a cross wind nine times out of ten the fry would head into the wind. So knowing that the first thing I did when arriving at the reservoir was to check the wind and position myself accordingly, but if the wind was blowing straight up or down the reservoir it was toss a coin time.

As the black cloud of fry moved down the bank over your baits you could almost guarantee a run, the pike and eels striking through the fry. Obtaining bait was no problem at the reservoir, all you had to do was run your landing net along the culvert wall, or use a drop net. Often you had to let half of them out so you could lift the net and you'd still be left with enough for a dozen sessions. It was all so easy, lots of runs, some nice doubles, the odd twenty, and no pressure. In those early years on Abberton there was only John and I, plus 'Irish Sean' and a young Max Bond who were putting any time on the reservoir. Later on, with Bernard I was to start fishing on Monday's while Sheila was noticing me coming home from Abberton with a grin on my face. "It's alright for you, out all day enjoying yourself" she moaned. Sheila was right, I was being a bit selfish it was Ford's shut-down and we were supposed to be on holiday. So I decided to take Sheila down to Abberton with me on my next trip, to have some of the action (I'm so good to her!). The alarm woke me up at 4.45, kicking Sheila out of bed I told her to put the kettle on and after a quick cuppa we were driving the thirty miles to Abberton. It had just gone six when I dropped the first bait out rightside of the culvert, and five minutes later the second bait was out on the left side. "Right Minnie, you can have all the runs, I'll be your gillie for the day", I tell her. I told you I was good to her (by the way "Minnie" is Sheila's nickname). "Min wake up, I said you can have all the runs", blimey she was asleep already!

Ten minutes later Min's into her first pike and I hand landed it, a fish of about 8lbs. As I'm re-baiting the other rod was away. "Get yourself around there and strike that run Min", I say as I re-cast. Five minutes pass and Min landed her first double of the day at 11½ lbs. The pike had wolfed the bait down and I had to go through the gill rakers with the forceps to unhook it. Casting out a fresh bait, putting the rod on the rests I went to clip the line into the indicator when it pings out of my fingers.

"Min get yourself out of that chair and strike this run", I shout. It's another small fish weighing about 5lbs; releasing it I re-cast, finally having both rods fishing again. Min pours herself a cup of tea when the right hand rod's away again. "Leave the tea and wind down to that fish", I tell her, the fish was in the culvert by now and going well. "Stop pussy footing about and get the pike off the bottom Min", I say getting agitated. "Don't you shout at me, what'd you think I'm trying to do", she replied. Finally, I slip the net under Min's second double, a fish of 14½ lbs. The sun is well up now and the runs start to dry up; two hours pass and Min lands another jack. At three o'clock Min has a little feeding burst, landing two jacks and a 13 pounder in quick succession. Again, the double has taken the bait well down and I had to go through the rakers. Min was striking instantly but its the third fish that had almost swallowed the bait, they certainly wanted it that day. Five o'clock and Min was looking at her watch, "What time are we going home Bill?", she asks. "Going home, we have nearly five hours of light yet, the best fishing's still to come", I tell her. Min starts to sulk and fidgets in her chair. "Min, left hand rod, Min, I said left hand rod, stop sulking and get out of the chair". She ignores me as she walks over to the rod and strikes. Going on to land another double. Six fish later, including her fifth double, we call it a day. We'd been fishing for 14½ hours and as I started to pack away I noticed a bit of a smile creep over Sheila's face. "Well what did you think of the day's fishing Min, fantastic, yeah?", I ask putting the last of the gear into the car. "Boring" she replied, "Boring, what'd you mean boring", I say. "Slow that's what I mean, bloody slow", she said. "Slow, you've just had a hatful of fish including five doubles, blimey some people fish all season for a catch like that in other parts of the country", I explain to her. "It was still slow, and another thing, I don't like the way you stuck those scissors in the pikes' earholes", she replied laying back into the car seat and shutting her eyes. "They were rakers not earholes and that's the best way to go with the forceps not scissors, when the fish is deeply hooked".

"Anyway did you enjoy your day out?", I ask. "No, I didn't think you were ever going home", she said. "Well you now know what I have to suffer every week", I tell her.

For the last twenty years Sheila's been as good as gold, not moaning about my fishing at all.

Apart from one small hiccup, around that time, I still hadn't sorted out a live bait tank since moving to Pitsea. I was keeping the baits in the bath, sometimes for days at a time - we must have been the dirtiest family in town. It all came to a head when Sheila wanted a bath and I'd got three big eels and a dozen roach in there. "Bill get these fish out of the bath", Sheila screams. "Where am I going to put them", I say. "I don't care what you do, how am I supposed to bath with them in there?", said Sheila.

"Can't you shoo them up one end", I say with tongue in cheek, Sheila was not amused.

It was August 1980, and I'd been back on Abberton now for four years. On arriving, I was greeted by 'Irish Sean', with only one other angler fishing, who turns out to be Mem Hassan. I was to learn later that day, Mem had been fishing the 'Big Pond with my old mates, Len and Jeff, and they had told Mem all about me. I also remember that day, sadly, because of the death of a big fish, the only one I know I've lost in the last 25 years.

Abberton at the time had a one rod rule, but when there were few anglers fishing we would sneak a second rod out. Laying it down in the grass nicking in a seagull's feather or a piece of silver paper on the line to act as a bite indicator. When we had a run the feather or paper would tear off down the concrete and into the water. An hour after starting, and no other anglers about I fitted up my second rod. Baiting up with a large pumped up bleak I dropped it out twenty yards along the bank. Laying the rod in the grass, clipping on a small piece of silver paper I opened the bale arm and tucked the line into a rubber band. Ten minutes passed and my 'sleeper's' away as the silver paper moved across the concrete in fits, stopping and starting, then disappearing down in the water. Striking into the fish it goes absolutely potty, I was playing it quite hard, but not gaining much line. Tail walking all over the reservoir after five minutes I had her close and after one more short run she was on the top ready for Sean to net. The single hook was in the scissors and dropped out easily. She weighed just under 25lbs and with a length of 44 inches. After a couple of photos she was back in the water. Mem and Sean congratulated me and we then settled back to our fishing. Suddenly there was a swirl on the surface ten yards out, it was my pike and she was clearly gassed up. Mem managed to re-net the fish and we staked her out in a large keepnet along side the culvert wall. For the next two hours I tended the pike, working up and down along the net. At long last she seemed to have recovered, crashing herself up against the net trying to get out. We decided she looked good enough to release for a second time. She swam off

Two days later my fish was found dead in the corner

Alas, dead Esox, I knew you well.

strongly, and for the rest of the day we kept our eyes peeled for her but thankfully she didn't turn up. I felt a lot better. It was a week later Mem phoned and told me the bad news. He had gone back to the reservoir two days later and had found my fish dead in the corner. Telling me he had cut the pikes head off, putting it in a bucket and hiding it behind the toilets, for me to pick up. If the wind had not been blowing into the road bank that day we would never have known it had died. We still haven't solved the problem of badly gassed fish, and need some research in this field.

Abberton has some massive bream, but in all my years fishing there I've only seen them twice. The first time was with John when we pre-baited on the 'natural side' in the close season, John going on to catch a tiddler of about 7lbs. The second time was in the evening a few years later, the light had nearly gone as I walked down to the toilet before going home. A big fish swirled just off the bank in the corner, then another one. Thinking they were pike I went back with a rod, twitching a dead bait through the shoal. I nearly fell in as bream well into doubles, rolled ten yards out in front of me. They were like dustbin lids, porpoising in the corner. I'd bet a bream angler would have given his right arm to have been fishing on that shoal that September night. Mem had fallen in love with Abberton, fishing with me more and more on the reservoir. I bought a second hand escort van, painted it bright yellow, and stenciled a four foot pike on either side. I know, I'm 40 years old, but pike fishing was taking over my life. Anyway the van had its advantages, no one would steal it, and I could see it a mile away in a full Tesco car park! Mind you it had its disadvantages too. There was the time I couldn't collect my strike pay at Fords. The pickets would not let me in, saying I'm not delivering fish while the factory's on strike! Then there was the time Sheila and I arrived at a holiday park for a weeks holiday. As we pulled inside the gates, an old dear taps on the van's window, "I'll have a nice piece of cod, young man, if you have it", she asks. I feel a sharp pain in my ribs as Sheila's arm slips as we drive away.

Back at Abberton, in the 1980 season there were a lot of big roach in the culvert some of them topping two pounds. I believe it was about three months after I lost my fish on the reservoir a small group of anglers had come to fish a pike match on the water. John and I fished the culvert one either side and we had landed one or two doubles before they turned up. The lads started their match, two hours passed and they hadn't caught anything at all. It was late afternoon when one of the anglers fishing halfway down on the left

Abberton Reservoir and a good fish from the 'small side'.

24lb 12oz and full of roach

Jeff Ducker and I sitting in one of Abberton's big fish traps, it's been removed for maintenmance work. 10 years later they were to be removed for good.

Low water levels but still catching

of the culvert got stuck into a decent fish. Five minutes later, with all his mates around him they finally net the fish. As they lifted it out and carried it up the bank, John and I went down to have a look. "It don't look too bad John, could be a twenty", I say. The other anglers are two deep around the fish as I poke my head in. Christ the fish is fat and I mean fat, its no more than 40 inches long built like a carp. There were bumps and bulges sticking out all along the pike's flank and on closer inspection the fish was crammed full of big roach. When weighed the pike went 32lbs. I couldn't believe it. I'd just witnessed my first thirty caught, and it shouldn't have weighed more than 22-24lbs. "Blimey", I think to myself, "what would some of the fish we've caught weigh after a feed like that?" With the big baits in the culvert it seemed to me it was all a matter of the luck of the draw. For example, say you hook a fish first thing in the morning at the start of its feeding spell and it weighs 25lbs. Now you don't hook the fish till after several hours of heavy feeding, the last bait it wants is yours, and the same fish might weigh thirty pounds. It was all looking good and it was only a couple of months later my day was to come. Mem had given me a large vaned float to try out on the reservoir. Vic Gibson and Eddie Turner had been experimenting with

Mem Hassan with a 20 pounder from Abberton Reservoir.

85

different designs and Mem had obtained a couple of them from Vic. They were certainly different with the long stem made up out of a quiver tip passing through a table tennis ball, sitting on top was a large vane. We had used the dart type float on Abberton for a long time, Colin Benbrook and Bernard having lots of fish. The only trouble with the dart float was, if there was a chop on the water they were not visible any distance out. With the Eddie and Vic floats the large vane was the breakthrough to their success; the vane certainly caught the wind and they stood out like a lighthouse well over 100 yards away.

I'm not a patient angler, I find it hard to sit behind a couple of deadbaits for any length of time. If I haven't had a fish after an hour or so, I'm re-casting or twitching the bait back, even moving on to another swim, with the Turner/Gibson drifter I was able to work at my fishing with my second rod, searching right out into the reservoir. As I work the float out it really gives me a buzz, seeing the big vane slip slowly beneath the waves, 150 yards from the bank. My first two sessions with the drifter I had only small fish apart from one good one that I pulled out of when the hooks turned into the bait. Later I was to find a bit of a hotspot on the right hand side of the culvert in the 'big side'. If the wind was right, being west or south west I could work my bait out 120 to 150 yards along the right hand bank and it would usually result in a run. It was off this bank I had pulled out of the good fish. I was using two singles at the time so a change to a couple of no.6 trebles was called for to use on my next visit to the reservoir on the coming Monday. It was the 9th February 1981 and I'll repeat what I wrote for the Anglers Mail on that date 15 years ago.

That day my son Bernard and I arrived at Abberton at 6.30 am and were greeted in the half light by Steve Richards. "How's it going mate?" I asked. With a big grin on his face he replied that he had already had one of 11lbs. Just then I noticed his rod was sliding down the rod rests and into the water by the culvert. "Steve, your rod" I said. Steve spun round running into the water, he just missed his rod so grabbing his other one he casts a lead across the fast disappearing butt and got a hold first time. He pulled the rod to the side and found that the line had blown round the reel handle when the pike had taken, and was still on. After a spirited five minute fight, I slipped the net under a nice fish of 18lbs. "You lucky so and so", I said picking up my gear, eager to get to my swim opposite the hotspot along the right hand side of the culvert. The forecast was for a west to north-west wind but at that moment what little wind that was blowing, was coming from the south. Two 10ft compound taper rods were quickly assembled and Mitchell reels fitted, one with 11lb line, the other with 9lb. A 11/2oz lead went on the 11lb line, a 5 inch roach lip-hooked on the 1/0 single and punched fifty yards straight out. I slipped one of the big vane floats onto the other rod and on the end went one of the traces with two no.6 trebles. Placing the rod in the rests I waited for the wind to freshen and hopefully swing west. Half an hour passed and the flag on the ledgered rod dropped to the ground. Striking instantly resulted in a jack of a couple of pounds. Bernard, who had positioned himself about 30 yards to the left of the culvert was also into a small fish. The next five hours passed quite slowly, the only run coming to Bernard who had another small fish on a float fished bait close in. The wind was still south and I was determined to get at least one bait out to the hotspot. Mounting the biggest roach I could find, I set the stop-knot at 13ft and cast out. Walking 10 yards along the bank I submerged the rod top and wound down sinking the line. With the rod top still under water and playing out the line I walked back to my original position. Now with the bow of line acting like a drag the float slowly headed straight out to the hotspot. It was about 120 yards out when the float disappeared. Quickly winding down until I could wind no more I set a nice bend in the rod. Steve had seen the float go, and with net in hand walked towards me. Twenty yards of line was easily recovered when the fish stopped swimming towards me and kited slowly to the right. All I could feel now was a heavy weight as I gradually gained line. Then, fifty yards out the rod was almost pulled from my hands as the pike made it's first blistering run. I frantically backwound as it made three more powerful runs. Thirty yards out she slowed and I started to lift her from the bottom. Like a submarine surfacing a back and then a fin appeared. I slowly eased it to the waiting net and, as it went across the arms I saw her girth. Then with a couple of flicks of her tail she was twenty yards out again. She came over the net a second time, Steve lifted, the big fish was mine. A canvas weigh bag comes from nowhere, Vic Gibson put scales into my hands and I lift 32lbs. "The weight of the bag", I cry. "One and a quarter", she's a thirty, a good thirty", came the reply. Photos and measurements were quickly taken, 43½ inches to fork of tail, 24½ inch girth. With her cradled in my arms I sat in the water and as I let her slip away, with a final wave of her tail she was gone. Years of fishing, thousands of rod hours and it was over in minutes. I hope pike anglers all over the country experience that wonderful feeling at least once in their lifetime. It had taken years for me to catch my first thirty, as I've just stated. In fact, although I've been pike fishing all my life it was ten years of concentrated effort from 1971 to 1981 before I reached my goal. In that time a few friends and I had put well over 100 twenties on the bank, and my thirty was only the second one I'd seen in all that time.

But well worth waiting for what an incredible high it gave me, it was like winning the pools. My mind was even going back to when I was a small boy with dimples, fishing the 'Ornamentals', and losing a big pike with my eyes full of tears. I promised myself "one day", and my day had certainly come at long last.

The 'drifters' were the business, catching us fish we weren't able to cover before. Drift fishing the 'big side' at Abberton we were dependent mainly on a west wind. Being restricted to the road bank it could be very frustrating at times. You've just worked your bait out and caught a nice double, re-baiting you cast out your drifter to go through the same area again, only for the wind to drop or swing to the north or east, making your drifter more or less redundant. I remember a time when the wind was in the south, blowing off the right hand side of the reservoir. I'd been waiting all morning for it to swing and in the end I could stand it no longer. So I did a naughty. Running along the right hand bank with my rod for 150 yards I cast out and then, paying out the line I walked back to the road bank. Within minutes of returning the big vane float had gone, winding down to the fish I soon landed a plump 18 pounder. Re-baited, I again ran alongside the reservoir only to hear footsteps behind me. It was Max Cottis with his rod in hand trying to keep up with me! Max is not slow to jump on a good thing and we went on to catch some good fish. I thought it would only be a matter of time before John the bailiff saw me so I had to devise a method to get my bait out 100 plus yards when the wind wasn't favourable. I finally came up with a pulley system, making a special rod rest up at work to take a piece of plastic air pipe, bent into a half circle. I then filled two deep reel spools with thread, that ran through the plastic air pipe which I had filled with grease. On the end of my drifter float I fixed a paperclip and I was ready to try it out on my next trip to Abberton. I arrived in the dark, so I could fit up my pulley system away from prying eyes. The wind was coming from the south east as I walked 150 yards along the right hand side of the reservoir carrying the special rod rest. Going down to the waters edge I pushed the rod rest well into one of the cracks of the reservoir's concrete banks. With a spool in either hand I paid

THE REDUNDANT PULLEY SYSTEM

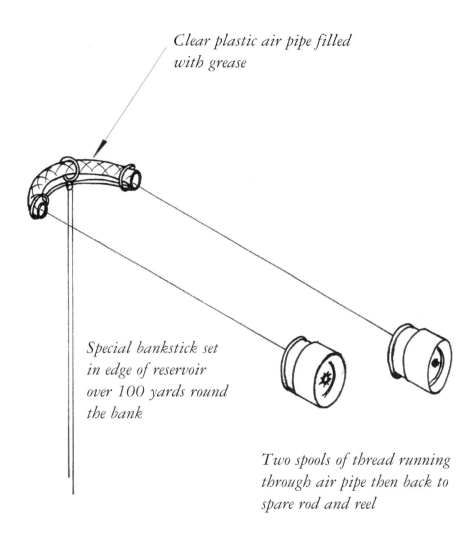

Clear plastic air pipe filled with grease

Special bankstick set in edge of reservoir over 100 yards round the bank

Two spools of thread running through air pipe then back to spare rod and reel

out the thread for thirty yards stopping to test the pulley, brilliant. I then carried on paying out the thread 'til I reached the road bank. I set up my rods about twenty yards from the corner, on the right hand side of the culvert making sure no other anglers can fish to the right of me. Making up a spare rod I put on the reel that was to take the two spools of thread I'd hidden under my bag. Okay all ready, on goes one of the spools on the spare rod, on the other I clip on my drifter to the thread.

Putting on a bait I placed the drifter rod in the rests and opened the bale arm. I then started to wind the thread around the air pipe 150 yards out along the reservoir's bank on the spare rod. The drifter float was slowly heading out against the wind, as the spool on the ground paid out the line. When it was 100 yards out I gave the drifter rod a flick, releasing the float from the thread. Success, the big vaned float started to drift away from the bank. I'd got my bait out over 100 yards in a cross wind, and I hadn't cast at all, the bonus being I had not damaged my bait. Now all I'll have to do when I want to run out another bait is to change the spool over on the spare rod. During the day, I caught several fish using the pulley and none of the other anglers fishing the reservoir suspected a thing. At the end of the day when it got dark I wound in my spools of thread and walked around the bank to recover my rod rest. In the next couple of months, using the pulley system about six times, I caught on every occasion, using it when the wind wasn't right. Then one day, arriving early to fit up my system after hearing the weather forecast, I couldn't help smiling to myself as I walked back to the road bank, knowing I'd got the edge on the other anglers. But was I in for a shock! As dawn came an angler launched the first model boat on Abberton making my pulley system obsolete in just two short months. With the arrival of the first model boats on the reservoir my pulley system wasn't the only thing to go, Vic Gibson and Rob were soon to follow. Talking about naughties, I'll have to hold my hand up to another little one I pulled at Abberton.

It was a time when the big pike were coming right up the culvert, feeding on the roach and bream fry. It paid you to have a bait in the culvert first thing in the morning and last thing at night. Putting your float and bait just under the road, the bigger the bait the better. It was during one of these feeding spells, I'd taken some nice fish in three days fishing that week, topped by two pike of 25 pounds plus. As the fishing was going so well, I decided to make a special effort to try and secure one side of the culvert for the coming

Saturday. Arriving at Abberton at 2.30 in the morning, there was already a van parked outside the reservoir gate. "Damn, I might as well have stayed in bed", I think, knowing that the occupants of the van would have the culvert well covered with their rod rests. The anglers in the van were members of a specimen group of that time and news of the pike in the culvert had certainly travelled fast. Sitting in the car I thought to myself "Why didn't I come down Friday night, instead of having those few hours sleep?" Oh well, I might as well check to see where the lads in the van are going to fish in the morning. Passing through the gate I look down either side of the culvert, both sides being well stitched up with rod rests, for about ten cracks along. Walking over the natural side, I climbed down onto the platform that goes over the fish traps in the culvert. There was a full moon reflecting off the water lighting up the culvert under the road. Suddenly there's an almighty crash as a pike strikes alongside the fish trap screen, frightening the life out of me. Then another, and another a little bit further under the road. The pike have the bream and roach fry penned up against the screen. Checking my watch it was 2.45, and we were not allowed on the reservoir 'til 7.30, although we normally start fishing from first light. Decisions, what's a full blooded pike angler to do in this circumstance? Just then hundreds of fry leap clear of the water as yet another pike swirls on the surface, making up my mind for me, as this poor pike angler succumbs to temptation. I was back on the platform with my gear in record time and as I tackled up a float rod I could hear the lads chatting and laughing in the van.

Putting on a 6oz roach I lowered it down onto a big swirl, the float cocked then disappeared. I wound the rod right down under the water and struck keeping a tight line on the fish with my rod still under water. I soon had it on the surface. Now the fun really started as my rod kept hitting the culvert roof, but surprisingly she slipped into the net quite easily. I was taken aback with the weight of the fish when I lifted her out. Grabbing my scales and weigh sling I carried the fish to the water's edge and weighed her at 27¼ lbs. I punched the air and go to let out a big shout but decided against it, not wanting to disturb the lads in the van! So I slipped her back eager to put another bait out. Dropping the float down alongside the fish trap screen the bait was off at 90 miles an hour. It was towing the float under the road, "Hang on that's not the bait it's a run". When I struck the fish was well down the culvert and I was having a lot of trouble bringing the pike back to the traps. Crashing and splashing about on the surface, after what seemed an

Abberton's culvert. Who's pulled the plug?

age, I finally handlined the pike into the net. Again, taking the fish down to the water to weigh she went 23½ lbs. Am I happy or what? Back at the car for a flask and to calm down a bit one of the anglers in the van got out to stretch his legs but after a few minutes returned, and resumed chatting and giggling with his mates. Checking my watch again it was 3.30. Reluctantly, I call it a night not wanting to give anything away or to be caught fishing in the dark. I left a couple of rod rests out on the natural side hoping the pike were still feeding against the traps in the morning. When dawn came the lads in the van were busy dropping their baits out all along the culvert, with no success the pike being long gone. After my experience of finding the pike feeding in the night I know I could have gone back for a repeat performance. But I didn't take advantage of the knowledge I gained that night, I'm just not that naughty. (If you believe that, then you'd believe anything!).

Going back to the vaned floats, after using those early ones I started to make my own. The body was made out of balsa wood about 4-5 inches long and as thick as a broomhandle. For the stem I used 12 inches of thin brass welding rod on the end of which I rolled a small piece of lead strip securing it with glue, a plastic vane made up the drifter. I used just enough lead to make the float self-cocking, painting the bottom half black and the top half fluorescent. When retrieving the big vaned float it would revolve slowly in the water. One day while rewinding my float after a 200 yard drift there was a big swirl on the surface 100 yards out, suddenly the rod went over and I was into a good fish. A minute later the fish let go and winding in, I saw the bait was unmarked but the float was wrecked. Two weeks later it happened again, this time I was reeling in quite fast 150 yards out when the rod slams over. The fish is big, no kicking of the rod top as I draw it towards the bank but again, after several minutes the pike let go. I'm cursing as I wind in the rest of my line - for the second time the bait wasn't touched, but there's not a lot left of the drifter. The balsa body was chewed up, the brass stem bent in three places, and the plastic vane missing. On closer inspection I find a big pike's tooth buried in the body of the float. The next month saw another couple of pike striking at the floats, and a young Wayne Sutton had his vane taken while he was drifting it out. It was happening too often to be a fluke, especially in the early part of the season. I thought it would be great to drift a livebait out just off the bottom for 200 yards, then have the drifter turn into some sort of surface plug, popping and diving as you wound in. I started to tinker about with a few bits and pieces, even putting a jointed body on one float with a couple of trebles. Unfortunately I never did get round to trying it out at the time, being side tracked into boat fishing. Perhaps I will in the near future, though there will be problems to solve with the floats no doubt. But that's what fishing is all about. I believe if you can get it right you'll certainly catch. Just ask the carp anglers of today, how many times their big marker floats have been attacked, when being retrieved fast across the surface. Just think, it's taken you half an hour to drift your bait out and it's going to take a coupled of minutes to rewind. Why not use those minutes to fish a gigantic surface lure back. It could be fun.

Going back to the model boats, after the appearance of the first one at Abberton, I just had to have one. I believe the early ones were made up by the carp boys to drop lots of boilies out, the possibilities and advantages to pike anglers looked endless. I continually pestered one of the welders at work, who was into model boats and planes. He finally sold me a fibreglass hull, receiver, transmitter and a small electric motor that ran a tiny propeller. He had removed the electric motor from a tug boat he had built. Giving me some help and instruction on how to set it up, I put it together. Two weeks of messing about at work, some more advice from my welder friend and the

The pike completely filled the large landing net.

It's a thirty. My day had certainly come along at last.

The arrival of the model boats making my pulley system obsolete.

25 pounds plus, it paid you to have a bait in the culvet first thing in the mornings and last thing at night.

boat was finally finished. I named it 'Henry', so called because it was conceived and built at Fords. Wayne Sutton and I took 'Henry' to Lakeside, to launch her maiden voyage. What a disaster! I didn't go mad on the first run out, dropping the bait only 50 yards then clipping my line into the bite indicator. 'Henry' was going round and round in circles over the top of my bait as I try to retrieve her, but she was not responding to the handset. I was shaking it violently when the alarm went off on my rod. Throwing the handset to Wayne I wound in a small fish. The boat had drifted almost to the far bank when at last I got control again, 'Henry' was heading home. 30 yards out a slight breeze came up and the boat was having trouble making headway against the wind. Wayne volunteered to walk round to pick it up. Lakeside at that time was an enormous building site and Wayne was having to climb over mountains of mud to reach 'Henry'. It was 15 minutes before Wayne returned with the boat and I decided not to chance it again until the wind dropped. An hour later the breeze died leaving a flat calm, so I launched 'Henry' for a second time. Again, only running it out for 50 yards I then tried to release the bait but it wouldn't move. Winding the boat in backwards and checking to see what had gone wrong, I found the hooks had caught the inside of the bait tube. Freeing the hooks I launched the boat yet again, success at last as I drop the bait down where I had the first fish. Pressing the switch to the right of the handset to turn the boat, 'Henry' carried straight on. Panicking I pressed the switch to the left, hoping to turn it the other way, no luck, 'Henry' was going full steam ahead. Stopping the boat, I wondered what to do next. Restarting 'Henry' I tried again to turn her but she was not having any of it. I thought the servo had packed up, so for the second time 'Henry' was drifting to the far side of the lake. At this point I renamed the bloody boat, "The Dagenham Dustbin". Poor old Wayne trudged off once more to retrieve the horrid little thing. It wasn't just teething troubles, the boat was useless. It sat too high in the water, the electric motor was not powerful enough, radio control faulty, and the servo mechanism had packed up. I had badly designed the bait release tube, in fact a load of crap.

Then as luck would have it, four weeks later I was to meet with Steve Wells and Tony Corless when fishing Lakeside again. I was later to find out that both Steve and Tony also worked, (I use the term 'worked' loosely) at Fords, Dagenham. Steve was also messing about with radio controlled boats at the time going on to make us two identical ones. The boats proved to be the most reliable and hardy I'd seen so far.

Model boats had certainly taken over at Abberton and we were dropping deadbaits out as far as the eye could see. I would also use mine to run out a drifter, even when the wind was blowing off the road bank, the reason being the bait wasn't stunned by casting.

Going back to the time when the pike were feeding in the culvert, with the removal of the fish traps the culvert never did fish as good again. Mind you I wasn't sorry to see them finally go. When Keith was the bailiff for the reservoir he would lift and empty the fish traps daily. If the bait was scarce we would cadge the odd roach from him. Any eels in the traps were thrown in the back of his Land Rover, the rest of the fish returned. After Keith had left the Water Company it was some time even weeks before somebody would come down to empty the traps. It was during that period, just as Abberton peaked, that I was hoping for one or two big fish before the season closed. For the last fortnight the reservoir had been fishing quite slow, and the particular day in question, I was on the natural side when an employee from the Water Company came down to empty the traps. Walking down to the culvert to have a look I was shocked as the traps came clear of the water. In all my time at Abberton it was the first time I've seen big pike in the traps. The doors on the side of the traps were opened to release the fish and as they wiggled their way back to the water I counted them out. There were nine in one and seven in the other, all big twenties with two possibly going over thirty pounds. A lot of the pikes' snouts were worn away, being in the traps for some time. No wonder we had found it slow, the pike we were after were already captured. It wasn't long after that incident stories were flying around that a syndicate had acquired some of the big Abberton pike for their small water, taking the very fish, a few dedicated anglers had spent the last few years fishing for. So you see, at the time I was glad to see the fish traps dismantled. Although the reservoir has had a few hiccups over the years, it doesn't take Abberton long to start to produce good fish again.

Most pike waters only last a few seasons but I believe Abberton will always do the business. The reservoir is quite unique with anglers only being able to fish a couple of hundred yards of road bank on 1200 acres of water. The pike move in, get caught once maybe twice, then move out not to be seen again for months, having literally hundreds of acres of safe water to lose themselves in. There is a lesson to be learned here and perhaps that is the way to run some pike waters in the future, giving the fish and water an extended rest? I haven't fished Abberton so much over the last 4-5 years, spending my time on the trout reservoirs and some of my local lakes although I do manage to fish there at least half a dozen times in a season. On one of my visits to Abberton just recently as I pulled up by the culvert a couple of anglers came up to greet me. "What's an old piker like you doing here Bill?", they ask. "What'd you mean old, and what I'm doing here is fishing", I replied. "Get out of it, you've come down to see if there's any bait in the culvert", they say.

"Yeah, that's it, you've come to nick some bait", piped in another. "No I'm fishing", I tell them again as I take my tackle out of the car. Walking over to the gate, I dropped my gear down alongside it and take a tape measure out of my pocket. Making sure the lads are watching, out of the corner of my eye I start to take measurements of the gate. With one hand on my chin, the other scratching my head, standing there I run the tape across the gate posts. At long last three of them walk over, as I'm making out to write some figures down on a piece of paper. "What you up to now Bill?", one asks. "Oh blimey, you've caught me", I say. "Caught you doing what?" he inquired. "Taking measurements of the width of the gate posts", I replied. "What you taking measurements for?", they ask. "To see if my zimmer frame will pass through the gate", I say laughing. Talking of zimmer frames, Sheila reckons she's going to have me cremated, then throw my ashes into Abberton's culvert when I die. Seriously though, Abberton will always have a place in my heart, it's where my dream came true.

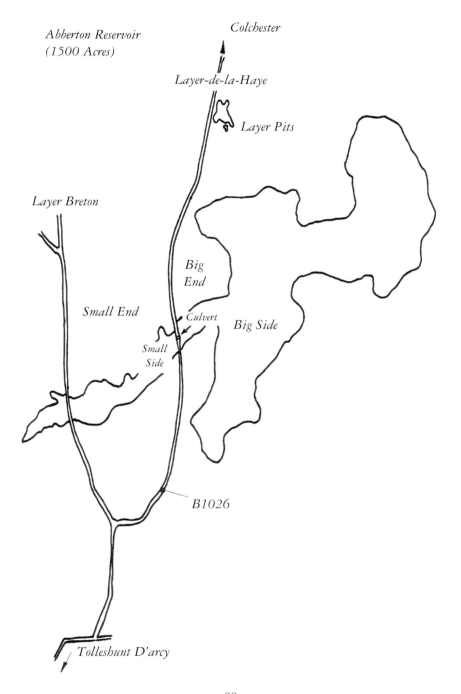

Abberton Reservoir
(1500 Acres)

Colchester

Layer-de-la-Haye

Layer Pits

Layer Breton

Big
End

Small End

Culvert

Big Side

Small
Side

B1026

Tolleshunt D'arcy

6

LAKESIDE

L akeside, Tescos, or as Eddie Turner called it "The Chalk Pit". This piece is just an update on what was once a fabulous water holding some huge pike.

I didn't fish the water myself until January 1989, the pit being well past its best by then, having only a few months there before Mick Toomer acquired the fishing rights in 1990. The last couple of years, I hadn't done a lot of fishing and I had mostly dropped out of the big fish scene. I even stopped buying the angling weeklies, so I couldn't be tempted. The reason being I was having to spend a lot more time at work, as my daughter and two sons had got themselves happily married.

It was Bernard who first told me about the place some years earlier. Working at Tescos at Pitsea as a bakery manager he was temporarily transferred to Thurrock Lakeside to help launch their new store. It was probably because Tesco was the first store to open at Lakeside, that the pit was named after the grocery firm. The staff at the new store told Bernard they had seen anglers fishing the chalk pit alongside, catching some big fish they believed might be pike. So Bernard, in his lunch breaks had a walk round the pit to see if he could fish it. Coming across some security guards he asked who he had to see for permission to fish there. The security guard told him he had no chance, what with all the building that was going to take place. The few anglers with permits on the water were fishing there to stop others from doing so.

Bernard told me what he had found out so I arranged a visit there with him to check it out. We parked the car and started to walk round the pit opposite Tescos where some small trees and bushes were sticking out of the water, the construction workers having backfilled right up to them. There were thousands of rudd darting in and out of the branches and after walking for about 50 yards I'd grown about 12" with the mud and chalk building up on my boots. With the big earth moving vehicles all over the place it looked like the surface of the moon. "Come on Bern, lets go back to the car, it don't look good with all this construction work going on", I say trying to pull my boot out of the mud. On the way home Bernard said he would give it a go for a few hours early Sunday morning with Wayne Sutton.

Unfortunately the part of the pit they decided to fish was the deep pool by the A13 road. After two hours they had a dozen jacks to about 7lbs and thinking that's what the staff at Tescos had seen they gave it up as a bad job, and came home. So for the next two years I'm happily driving past the pit twice a day as I go back and forth to work at Dagenham. It wasn't until December 1988, fishing with Wayne at Abberton somebody let it slip that Eddie had caught some big thirties at Tescos. Wayne went a ghostly shade of white "Bill, I can fish at Lakeside as my cousin Barry's relations run the security on the site". Barry asked me if I would like to fish it with him. I told him me and Bernard had already fished there and it wasn't worth the

Bushes sticking out of the water.

102

effort being full of jacks.

Wayne got in touch with Barry and they started to fish Tescos at every opportunity. Barry being mainly a match angler, Wayne soon put him right on the finer arts of pike fishing. What a teacher Wayne turned out to be, in the next five trips Barry took three thirties from the pit! I believe Barry had only caught about 12 doubles in his life, but what doubles, three of them going over thirty pounds from Tescos, a 25lb plus from Abberton and a 25lb plus from Dartford in Kent.

I was breaking my neck to get on the water. Finally with Barry and Wayne established on the pit I had a chance to fish. My first trip I set up by the offices, the level of the pit being still low. Fishing with four rods I put out an assortment of lives and deads. Within minutes I had three of the rods out of the water and for the rest of the day I only fished two, as the runs came thick and fast. No big fish but lots of action with pike up to 15lbs. A few weeks later fishing with Wayne and Barry at Lakeside, we were to meet up with Tony Corless and Steve Wells. That day I was to see my first and last Tesco thirty. Barry having his third one from off the offices, and Tony also landing his third thirty from the other end of the pit alongside a small Island. The season ended for us with no more big fish landed. Teaming up with Steve we were looking forward to fishing the pit in the new season and Steve and I decided to have a go for the big crucian carp that lived in the chalk pit. So, on the run up to the 16th June 1989 we put in some bread and corn on the way home from work. Fishing just right of the offices in 12 feet of water we had crucians up to 3lbs. Four pound fish were definitely on the cards as we saw a lot of bigger fish roll. Unfortunately for us we never did get a chance to find out, it all coming to an end when Lakeside management gave Mick Toomer the fishing rights, but only for the deep pool at the A13 road end, leaving the best part of the pit out of bounds.

Roy Lyons and my old mate Colin Benbrook had permission to fish on a small piece of land either side of the offices and carried on fishing there for another year. Roy had a nice fish of 29lbs plus and a little while later that year a young lad landed it again at a whopping 35lbs. We believe it was possibly the last big fish in the pit with Roy and Colin's fishing finally coming to an end with the arrival of the scuba divers at Lakeside. They ran a string of cork floats across the front of the offices, from there to the island finally going onto the other side of the pit. The floats marked the boundary between the anglers and scuba divers.

Wayne Sutton with a 22 pounder.

(Easy), Barry Sutton with his third thirty from Tescos.

Talking to Steve and Tony, on Eddie's and Keith Howard's fantastic catches of big pike on the Pit, I told them how sad I was on missing out on some truly massive pike. Tony said he had also missed out, having caught the very same fish a year or two earlier at lower weights. He also told me he had one thirty that Eddie hadn't caught, being on his living room wall.

Tony went on, there was also one other thirty found dead that year. "I first fished the water in September 1986" Tony said, "after getting a letter giving permission from Ray Pledger, whom I'd met at a party some time before".

"He told me that he wasn't an angler and didn't have a clue what the pit held. At that time virtually nobody else was fishing the lake, it being very strictly policed by the security and site workers, who become a bloody nuisance, asking who you were every time I fish the place, which was a lot at the time". Anyway, on my first trip, which was no more than a couple of hours after work one evening, I took a fish of 21lbs on a spinner and a smaller fish. That whetted my appetite somewhat, as you can imagine, so the next week I returned with a plentiful supply of clonking great rudd livebaits. Taking a thirty on my very first cast, followed by a host of other fish.

The thirty's the fish I had stuffed as you know, no apologies to anyone as I regarded the place as "my" water. I didn't think it had anything to do with anyone else and still don't, anyway I digress.

Further trips produced more and more fish, although no more monsters that season. Colin Benbrook and Steve Wells joined me on the water shortly after I had the thirty, usually one at a time, at first as I was a bit wary of taking guests. We had some great sport for the rest of the season, taking some massive bags of fish, forty fish in a morning not being unusual but no more really big fish.

The following season they started to backfill the lake, the water in the main body of the pit looked literally like milk with the chalk. Although we did fish the 'bowl' end of the lake quite a bit, taking again very large bags of fish.

We then moved off the water for a while and fished Cottons Farm, a water on which for once I enjoyed considerable success. Taking half a dozen twenties to 30¼lbs in weight in only 8 trips, not bad going for me considering I wasn't even a member at the time.

Anyhow, the following season 1988 we moved back onto Tescos and started to fish the main body of the lake again. We start to catch some big fish, high twenties, culminating for me in December '88 with a fish of 32¼ lbs. Steve also took a thirty although Colin never did get one, coming close though with 28½ lbs. With the turn of the year came another thirty in January 1989, you remember this fish because as I was playing it you come walking down Bill.

"Oh dear" I said to Steve, just what you don't want some good looking bloke clocking you with a thirty. Anyway, he eventually landed the fish and distinctly remembers telling this ugly looking bloke (thanks mate) that the water was finished. I don't think you believed us somehow especially when Wayne's mate got another thirty later that day under the offices, where you were all fishing that day Bill.

That's the day we all met if you remember, anyhow that was the last of the big fish. Shortly after that we heard that the fish had all been nicked but, not wanting to believe it we continued to fish the water for the rest of the season and the next. But eventually with no more of the very big fish coming, we had to accept it.

"We were all a bit choked about it as you know, but nothing ever lasts for long does it Bill? To get a few good seasons out of a water isn't bad going. I often look back on those few short seasons and all the big fish that we took and have to pinch myself and have yet another look at the photos, before I can convince myself it wasn't all a dream.

After this they fished various waters in the Fens and Broads, before discovering Ardleigh and your the last bloke I need to tell about all that has subsequently happened there. I've still to get my Ardleigh thirty, having to make do with as you know Bill a couple of 29 somethings.

Still you wait mate, this season I'm going to nail one (I say that every year) mind you it's great fun trying. Just a bit more about Tescos, it was strange Bill that in the first couple of seasons, runs on salt baits were about as rare as Colin getting the first round in. Dead naturals producing plenty of runs especially pumped up, and another thing was that you wouldn't get a run at first light. About quarter to eight it was like a switch being thrown, with all the rods flying at once. Then about 12.30 the switch was thrown again and although we often fished into dark, rarely did we get another pull.

When you come onto the water Bill all that changed with runs coming at anytime and sometimes all the time! As for bait, I often think they would have taken a pork sausage if you'd have chucked one out at that time. For the record, we think the water held originally nine different thirties, one or two not quite making the mark until the backend. I think that between us we

30 pounds Tesco 86 one that Eddie didn't catch.

Tony Corless with a 32¼ pounder form Tescos in 1988.

caught them all, quite amazing for a wild water. Before it was backfilled it held vast shoals of really massive Rudd, really big fish they were, you would often see great shoals of them rolling like bloody big bream at first light. The last time I saw them was when the water was like milk and they were all rolling around the edges of the pit in distress.

I think they nearly all died at that time, which was a shame, as doubtless they and the big Crucians were what grew so many of the pits pike to a large size. They were really beautiful fish, four pounders amongst them without a doubt.

That describes Tony's time on Tescos, I feel really sorry for him missing out when the pit was reduced in size and the pike packed on all that weight, leaving Eddie and Keith Howard to clean up while Tony was having to make do with half a dozen twenties to 30¼lbs from across the river at Cotton Farm. Honestly, I do feel sorry for him, (what did he call me that ugly bloke when we first met), I could do with missing out myself like that with half a dozen twenties to 30¼lbs in only eight trips!

It was a year or so later in early April 1993 I received a phone call from Mick Toomer telling me after a three month search for some big pike, he had finally succeeded in finding some - three enormous specimens weighing in at 31lbs, 36lbs and 38lbs. They were supplied by Framlingham Fisheries who had netted them from Grafham Water earlier in the day. He told me he had put them into Lakeside to boost the big pike population there. As the big outsize specimens were being released into their new home Mick had video'd them and asked me if I was interested in seeing it. Picking up Bernard we drove round to Micks to see the video of the big fish going into Tescos. I watched with mixed feelings, being a bit sad that these magnificent fish had been removed from their large reservoir home. The only consolation being they were going into a water with a proven track record for producing big pike, far better than a fishmongers' slab or a hole in the ground. The 38lb was one beautiful fish and I decided there and then to try and catch it in five months time when Mick opened up Lakeside for pike fishing. I just might catch my Tescos thirty yet. Around about the same time as Mick had put his pike into Tescos a good friend had also received some big pike from Framlingham Fisheries. They also had been netted from the big trout reservoir Grafham Water. These fish were stocked into a complex of small lakes in Norfolk and the fish were also big weighing 31lbs, 33lbs, 37lbs and a massive 38½ pounder.

The lakes were to be fed with a regular stocking of trout to feed the pike and it was to be interesting to see the outcome from the two stockings of pike, in the months to come. September arrived and Steve, Bernard and I were spending a fair amount of time on one of our local waters the 'Warren'. After catching a twenty before I had to go to work one morning, I was well pleased.

Later that day as I packed my gear away in my fishing room, I noticed the picture of the big Grafham pike on the wall. Sticking it there five months earlier, like a wanted poster, to remind me about the big fish Mick had put

Mick Toomer with a 27lb from Lakeside.

into Tescos. That was the fish I would be gunning for.

Phoning Steve I asked him if he fancied fishing Tescos for a couple of hours in the morning before we went to work. Steve agreed, so I arranged to meet him at Lakeside, in the car park at 6 o'clock opposite the offices, and to bring his model boat with him. Setting up drifter rods Steve and I ran our baits 80 yards down the pit with radio controlled boats but before we had run our second rods out the big vaned floats had disappeared, both rods were away. Winding down together we struck but after a few seconds I pulled out while Steve went on to land a fish of about 8lbs. Putting on another bait I ran the boat out to where we had the first two takes. The boat was only halfway back when again the vane dips then shoots away. Setting the hooks the fish stays deep. "This feels like a good fish Steve", I say as it plods slowly up and down in front of the offices. A minute or two later she surfaces in front of us. "Blimey it looks like one of the Grafham fish", I whisper not wanting to frighten it as she slips into the net. It's a big framed fish, eagerly I go for the weigh sling and scales to see if she will reach the magic mark. As I slip her into the sling I notice how empty the pike was, and as I lift her off the ground she starts to kick, finally the dial settles 26lbs 2ozs. It's been nearly three years since Steve and I had come off Tescos, and I thought I'd cracked it first time back. Disappointed, I turn to Steve "Oh well, I reckon

Pictured left to right: 36lbs, 32lbs and 38lbs.

she'll be a good thirty later in the year mate".

When I checked the photos it turned out the fish was the 38 pounder, the very fish I'd set my heart on catching, landing it on my second cast. Sadly, she had lost almost 12lbs in weight in just five short months, admittedly some being spawn, but still a very big weight loss.

Shortly after, our friend in Norfolk invited Steve to have a go for the Grafham pike that he had stocked into his waters. Steve jumped at the chance and went on to land a fish of 29lbs 14ozs. Again, checking photos it turns out to be the 33lb fish. With the regular stocking of trout to feed the pike it seems the Grafham fish were doing a bit better in Norfolk. Unfortunately not for long though, as time went on our friend was to lose the 31lb, the 33lb that Steve had caught at 29lb, plus the massive 38½ pounder. Perhaps the stress and upheaval of being moved and put into a new home is just too much for these big trout water pike. One good thing to come out of the stocking is that the original resident pike that live in our friend's water are packing on the weight. Taking full advantage of all the trout going in, one particular fish went from 20lbs to over 26lbs in a year.

Perhaps it might be better to stock with say, small doubles in future, the younger fish might stand a better chance, leaving the big pike where they are. Maybe in time the people running the big trout waters will finally realise what a valuable source of income the big pike could generate.

Mick put a second stocking of pike from Grafham into Lakeside with three more thirties up to 34lbs making a total of 6. I asked Mick how many he reckons have died, he told me as far as he knows only one. Although with fishing only allowed in the deep pool, I told Mick I believed he could have lost one or two more in the main lake. Also the Grafham thirties that may be left have probably gone back and wouldn't make that weight again. After saying that Mick has certainly made an awful lot of pike anglers happy landing their personal bests at Lakeside. But what about the original pike stock in Tescos? Well that's another matter! I believe some could come through to be very big again if one or two are not big already. With anglers being restricted to the deep pool the pike have a lot of safe water in the main lake and with all the underwater construction to support the landing stages and diving platforms a lot of bait fish congregate around the structures, the big fish laying underneath don't have to move far for their dinner. The best chance the anglers have is if the bait fish move down to the pool, drawing the big pike with them, or if one of the big fish strays down the main lake too far.

Going back to the very early days at Lakeside, I asked Gordon Edwards, (who is now one of the bailiffs on the Warren) what he could recall about his time on the chalk pit. Gordon was one of the construction workers at

Lakeside, (it was probably Gordon who gave Tony some grief when he fished there). Gordon told me he had also done some pike fishing at Lakeside landing fish to a weight of 34lbs. Then, as they backfilled he found he was spending more and more time rescuing fish from the small pools that were left, and carrying some enormous pike over to the main part of the pit, clearing all the mud and chalk from their gills and rakers, before releasing them (well done mate).

I can't end this chapter on Tescos without mentioning all the sightings and rumours from anglers and divers alike, of one gigantic pike nicknamed Arthur. What a stupid name for a girl if she exists, far better something like Big Bertha (all big pike are girls). Anyway, speaking to Mick about the fish he assured me its genuine having seen it himself on a couple of occasions. I asked Mick what he thought the pike might weigh, and though he wouldn't commit himself to a precise weight we were talking 'forties'. Mick has held some big pike in his time so he had a fair idea when he estimated the size of this pike. He said Arthur would suddenly turn up in the pool, with half a dozen sightings. Anglers would be playing in a jack when Arthur would come up and seize it, or follow it right in. Sometimes grabbing fish weighing as much as 10lbs swimming around for a while with it across its jaws then letting it go. This would go on for a week or two then Arthur would disappear again for months Mick said he could always tell when an angler had seen Arthur. As he walked around the lake an angler would come up to him and say "I've seen Arthur, Mick". "No you haven't" I would tell him. Then another might say, "Mick I've just had Arthur on". "I don't think so" Mick would reply. Then from time to time, he would come across an angler in quite a distressed state, he would be as white as a ghost. As he approached he would try to tell him something, the mouth was working but nothing was coming out and as he left him standing there gibbering, he knew he had seen Arthur!

112

Roy Wheeler displaying the 38lb pike in all it's glory before being introduced to Lakeside.

When I checked the photos it turned out the fish was the 38lb, the very fish I'd set my heart on catching, landing it on my second cast.

114

7

BOAT FISHING, TACKLE AND METHODS

It is probably fair to say in the last five years 75% of my pike fishing has been from boats, mainly on the big trout reservoirs. It has become the way of so much modern pike fishing that no-one seeking success can afford to ignore it.

FLOAT TROLLING

My favourite boat fishing method. Here is a brief description of the tackle I use:-

Rods - I make up four, both sets of rods have cork handles. With cork if a rod accidentally goes over the side it floats saving you an expensive accident.

Reels - Shimano GT 4500 and Daiwa BR 2050 bait runners.

Line - 15lb big game in "solar" green. Being highly visible it helps to prevent tangles, especially when there are two anglers in the boat and four rods in use. There are also some very good braids coming on to the market now, and which need looking at.

Floats - Different sizes of tubed sliders. I usually make my own, but there are plenty of good ones in tackle shops. I make up two rods with big floats, and two with medium so I can quickly change over rods to suit the size of baits.

Landing Net - When fishing alone it's best to have your net made up ready, with a friend aboard a net can be stowed away until needed. Push some wine corks or polystyrene up the handle so again, if it goes over the side you won't lose it.

TERMINAL TACKLE

Traces - 20" of 28lb wire, two no. 6 semi-barbless trebles. I paint the bend of the barbed treble with fluorescent or luminous paint to make hooking up baits in the half light easier, (I'm going blind in my old age). There is nothing worse than casting a bait off or checking a rod after an hours trolling only to find the bait has gone. Also the paint on the hooks makes the bait more visible to the pike resulting in more takes.

LOCATION

As with all fishing, if you don't locate you don't catch, it's as simple as that. Using an echo sounder cuts out a lot of the work, though even without one it's surprising how quickly you can map out even big waters in your head. Note features - shelves, drop offs, bait-fish and most important of all depth. Remember where you had runs from, use landmarks for positioning.

It soon becomes apparent, after a few sessions on a new water that there are hot areas as well as a lot of barren water.

So, with only a limited amount of time you can maximise your fishing to the productive areas. When trolling remember to alter the depth of the floats. One hotspot can be 30 feet deep the next at 8 feet. With the information you have stored in your head the depth can be changed and back out again in plenty of time before entering the next hot area.

As you go through, just check with the sounder that you have the depth right. A lot of anglers go out, find the average depth, then set their floats for the day. Don't forget when trolling the margins with a space of about 30' between the inside rod and the outside rod, the inside rod could be fishing in 6' while the outside rod might be fishing in 15', so set your floats accordingly.

PLOTTING UP (ANCHORING UP)

There will be times when the wind becomes too strong for trolling and you have to anchor (or "plot up", as I say). There are also days when it can actually out fish the troll. I'll give you an instance. Steve Wells and I decided to each take a boat out, the plan being with two boats we would find the fish quicker. The weather was perfect for trolling, hardly any wind at all, in fact a day all boat anglers dream of. Slowly trolling through the first productive area we both had a take instantaneously resulting in two nice doubles. Three more trolls through the area brought no response so I moved on. Steve found some bait-fish on his sounder and plotted up on them for a while. I continued trolling down the reservoir. After about two hours I'd had four more doubles up to 18½ pounds and three smaller fish.

"What a brilliant day I'm having", I think, as I notice Steve's boat heading towards me. "How's it going Steve" I shout across then I see that silly grin on his face, always a bad sign. "O'er I've just had six big doubles, and three twenties. I got the twenties sacked up, come and do the photos". So if you find a concentration of bait-fish it sometimes pays to plot up on them for a while!

Using the knowledge you have gained from your fish finder, anchor up wind off your chosen area at the deepest point if possible. If you have just come off the troll it's important when setting the depth of the floats to reposition the hooks in the baits. They will work 100% better when hooked dorsal and flank. Now with the wind behind you, and a greased line let your baits drift into the hotspot. When the float starts to drag, shallow up a foot and run them out again until all the area has been covered.

DEPTH

Back on to depth again, it is surprising how wrong you can get it when fishing deep water. You check your sounder at 32' and start to count the feet off, as you slide your stop knot up the line: 9 times out of 10 you will be several feet out either way. I don't take chances. I use a 3oz lead with a thick elastic band through it and even with a bait on the hooks I can still stick a barb into the band and set the float 6 inches off the bottom. It can make all the difference.

ELECTRIC TROLLING MOTORS

Not a necessity but again like the echo sounder can take a lot of the hard work out of your fishing, making it a lot more enjoyable. I use a Minn-Kota electric trolling motor and after three years hard work it hasn't let me down. With a fully charged battery you can troll for miles all day long. Although I had to pull the oars on my first few years fishing from a boat, I don't think I've caught anymore fish when using the trolling motor. In fact I found it actually paid to row sometimes, disturbing the water with the oars, making lethargic pike feed.

Saying that though, there is no way I'm going back on the oars at my time of life!

SAFETY

How much is your life worth? Fishing over deep water on the big lochs, rivers and reservoirs, wearing extra layers of clothing and moonboots if you go over the side in the depths of winter you stand no chance. I've got to hold my hand up and say that I was guilty in the past, thinking it won't happen to me. Then a couple of years ago I was caught out on Loch Lomond in a big blow and it frightened the living daylights out of me. Nowadays I always wear a flotation suit whenever boat fishing, being part of my clothing I don't forget to put it on! There are also some very good life jackets on the market now, small and compact you don't know you're wearing them. For the sake of your family and a few pounds they are a must.

WELFARE OF THE PIKE

Make sure you have something soft to lay your pike on. A good unhooking mat, even a piece of carpet or foam on the bottom of the boat will do. If fishing alone and you are unfortunate to have a deeply hooked pike it might pay you to leave it in the net and drift to the bank, giving you more room and stability to remove the hooks. If you don't want to weigh or photo a fish a lot of them can be lifted up by hand and unhooked in the water alongside the boat.

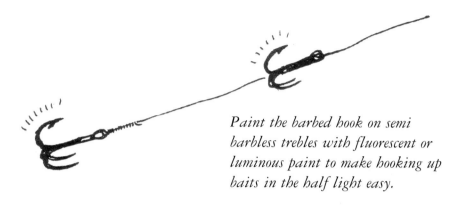

Paint the barbed hook on semi barbless trebles with fluorescent or luminous paint to make hooking up baits in the half light easy.

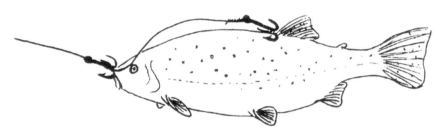

Hook up for float trolling.

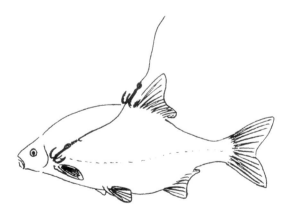

Hook up dorsal and flank when at anchor.

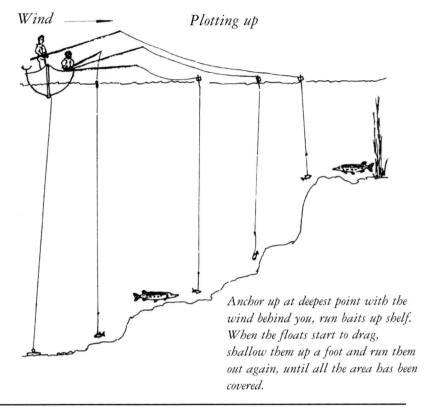

Wind ———►   *Plotting up*

Anchor up at deepest point with the wind behind you, run baits up shelf. When the floats start to drag, shallow them up a foot and run them out again, until all the area has been covered.

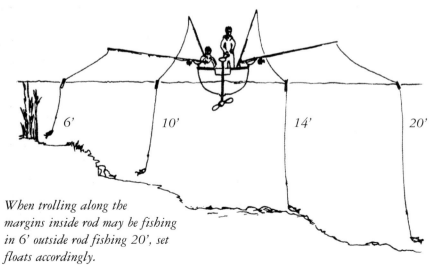

6'   10'   14'   20'

When trolling along the margins inside rod may be fishing in 6' outside rod fishing 20', set floats accordingly.

8

TROUT WATER PIKE FISHNG
ARDLEIGH RESERVOIR

Ardleigh first opened for fishing on the 14th September 1971. Situated near Colchester in Essex, it comprises 128 acres with a maximum capacity of 482 million gallons of water. I first got to hear about it while fishing Abberton with John Meecham in the '80's. One or two anglers had trout fished there and told us pike were attacking the trout as they played them in. John subsequently made a few inquiries at Ardleigh and was given a couple of booklets with information and regulations on trout fishing the reservoir. I made some inquiries of my own, continually pestering the Essex fisheries officer who used to visit Abberton when the traps were lifted. He told me it wasn't worth pike fishing as they had netted Ardleigh on several occasions and the biggest pike that turned up in the nets was a fish of 18 pounds. John and I decided that, on the information obtained we would give Ardleigh a miss and carry on fishing Abberton, although we would keep Ardleigh in our minds for the future.

A year later, 1987 we were to be blown away to read in the angling press of a massive fish caught by Mick Linton from Ardleigh, weighing a mind boggling 44lbs 14ozs and a new British record.

So much for the bum information I received, it was pointless tearing down there after the horse had bolted. For the next few months wouldn't every pike angler and their mothers be fishing it?

So I carried on fishing Abberton and my local waters for the next couple of years having good sport with fish to over twenty pounds. The only anglers I knew at the time fishing Ardleigh were Vince DuBerry and Terry Hunt. I first met Vince and Terry at Abberton, and two very keen pike anglers they were - blimey looking back I think they were probably madder than me. I

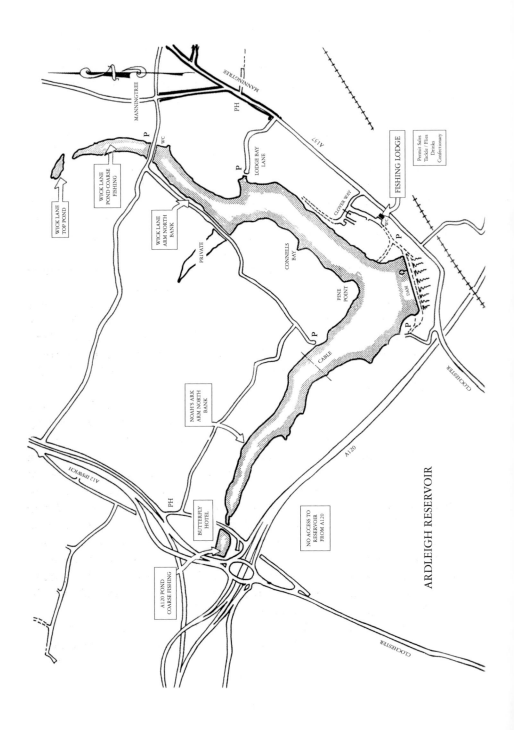

ARDLEIGH RESERVOIR

can remember a day when Wayne Sutton and I were making our way to Abberton. It had been a bitter cold night, and driving was a nightmare as the roads were a sheet of ice, and a blizzard was starting to blow. As I reached Maldon the snow was coming down so hard you couldn't see more than a couple of feet and the wipers were having trouble clearing the snow from the windscreen. Turning to Wayne I said, "I'm turning back mate, we must be the only ones stupid enough to be out on a day like this with the amount of snow coming down we could be snowed in for days". Unfortunately I was descending the big hill in Maldon at the time and how I reached the bottom without hitting anything I'll never know. With no control over the car at all, Christ knows what would have happened if I had touched the brakes. There was no way I was going to get back up the hill. "Looks like we are going to fish after all mate", I tell Wayne. "The one good thing is we will have the reservoir to ourselves, you can have the culvert".

The next ten miles took an age but finally we reached the road running over the reservoir. "Blimey there's a car parked by the gate".

I pulled up behind it as two figures stood up covered in snow. It was Vince and Terry looking absolutely blue, their cars ticking over as they were trying to defrost a gas bottle on the exhaust pipe to make a cup of tea. They had been there all night; their rod rests stuck in the cracks of the reservoir looked like tree trunks with the build up of ice. How they had survived the night I'll never know.

Vince and Terry were doing some fishing on Ardleigh, Vince had actually fished it a week or two before the record came out and had carried on fishing it. They were catching lots of doubles with only one or two twenties. I believe Vince and Terry had about 70 doubles each that year. Apart from Mick Linton's fish there were no more really big fish caught, the water company was still netting the reservoir and transporting the pike to Abberton. When the transporter turned up at Abberton we would all help to unload the fish although I didn't think Abberton needed the excess pike. Vince would go and sulk in one of the corners and have the hump for the rest of the day. I was interested to see the size of the fish they had netted but apart from one going 23lbs most of the fish I saw in 3 loads were small. So it wasn't until 1990 I was to have my first trip to Ardleigh. Steve had fished it the week before with Tony and had a low twenty.

I decided then it was about time I had a look at this reservoir so Tony booked me a boat for the following week. It seemed strange fishing from a boat, it being a long time since I had done so. The west arm was the hot spot I was told, fishing by the trout holding cages. So here I was rowing like mad trying to keep up with Tony and Steve. Three times I pulled out of the rowlocks falling back on my bum with my feet in the air. Mind you it didn't take me long to get a grip of this boating lark and I was soon leaving 90% of the other anglers in my wake. Not bad for a 50 year old. That first trip to Ardleigh was very slow, Steve, Tony and I didn't get a run for six hours of hard fishing. Then in the late afternoon Tony decided to move away from the trout cage.

I watched him pull out of the bay trolling his big vaned floats behind him, suddenly one just disappeared. Tony struck and the rod went right over as he refused to give line (I don't believe Tony ever gives line). Lifting the mud weight I went towards him as a big fish slipped into his net. Steve had seen the fight and joined me as we rowed to the bank together, leaving our baits fishing 30 yards out. On the bank the unhooking gear and cameras were placed on the grass, as Tony lifts the net and fish out of the water. As he lowered it on to the unhooking mat, I look at Steve, blimey it could be a thirty. The dial settles at 29lbs. "Nice one" I say to Tony congratulating him as I whip off his hat and stamp up and down on it into the mud.

As we tidy up I noticed one of my floats was missing and I run to the boat and strike, the rod's just tapping as I wind in. "What you got", Steve asks. "Just a tiddler", I replied as the vane surfaced a couple of yards out followed by a good perch. My first Ardleigh fish was a two pound perch and it had taken a small carp. Seeing Tony's fish I decide to spend a bit more time on Ardleigh, there just might be one or two more big fish coming through. Three trips later with a fair number of doubles landed I was to catch my first Ardleigh twenty.

Steve and I had plotted up (anchored) in the bay down the west arm. With the wind blowing into the bay, using a drifter I was running my baits on to the marginal shelf. Working hard I was constantly changing the depth of the floats as I fished them closer and closer to the bank. At long last one of the vanes dipped a couple of times then started to run towards me against the wind. Winding down, I pulled into the fish. It was soon alongside the boat, netting it I swing it aboard. "It looks close", I think to myself, as I slip it into the weigh sling and lift. "How big" Steve shouts. I punch the air "20½ lbs", I tell him. I slip her into a keep sack for Steve to photo my first Ardleigh twenty and as I tidy the boat up, I re-cast the rod with another bait.

I row to the bank not to photo my first twenty, but a brace.

Steve and I with twenties.

As I start to pull up the anchor to drift over to Steve the same float stabs down again. Two minutes later my second twenty's in the boat, two twenties in successive casts. Sacking her up with the first one I row to the bank with Steve, not to record my first twenty but a brace!

The season comes to an end far too quickly, Steve and I landing several more twenties from the reservoir. Just before the start of the 1991 season Steve said he would like to catch 5 twenties in the coming year as the best he had managed so far was four. It had been a long time since I'd chased numbers, not being interested in doing so having landed more twenties than I'm probably entitled to over the years. But Steve's enthusiasm was rubbing off on me, so with tongue in cheek I said, "Why stop at five mate, let's go for ten with 50 doubles". What with all the trout waters opening up, dates on Llandegfedd, Bewl water, Bough Beech and others plus all our local pits and not forgetting Abberton, "It will be a piece of cake", I tell him.

The start of the 1991-92 season found me stalking carp on my local waters, I always like to start my season off with a carp or two. Catching them on the float or taking them from the top after a couple of weeks and with a dozen doubles under my belt I have the carp bug out of my system. I can now get down to the task ahead; some serious pike fishing. The venue we start our campaign on is a large pit in Suffolk, Steve talks me into night fishing it. Blimey I don't even night fish for carp these days!

With the pike target I've set for Steve and myself I thought I'd better put some hours in though. The pit was a good doubles water with an outside chance of a twenty. Using our model boats we dropped our baits (large lives and pumped up deads) to the edge of some sunken trees. Two hours into dark I have my only run of the night resulting in a nice double weighing 13lbs. Dawn breaks, I wind in one of the deadbait rods and fit it up with a drifter. Nicking on one of the large livebaits I boat it out to the edge of the trees. The bait was taken before I retrieve my boat, and in the next three hours I land six more fish with two of them going into double figures, both breaking 15lbs. So my first pike session of 1991 ends with 3 doubles. I'm well pleased, a very good start, the show is well and truly on the road. Working shifts I was able to have a few hours on Abberton before and after work, picking up the odd double now and again, to add to my total. The weekends would find me back on the Suffolk water, three trips later with the water level dropping drastically I pull off after losing some good fish in the more exposed trees. I didn't just want to catch at any cost, being too much for the pike to

126

pay.

August arrived and Steve and I were looking forward to fishing Llandegfedd for a week. It was the first time the Welsh water had opened up in summer, so perhaps we'll stand a chance with lures?

We had secured two bookings running consecutively with another two days in October. But what a let down! The temperature was in the eighties all week, we were starting on the water two hours too late and coming off two hours too early. After casting lumps of metal and wood around for five days without a fish it was enough to put you off spinning for life. Mind you I did stick at it and I had two chances, one when a very big fish followed a small Voblex right to the boat turning away only when I stopped winding, as I froze on seeing the fish. The second time was on the third day out and my concentration had lapsed. I had cast my lure across one of the buoy anchor ropes in 40 feet of water. There was no way I was going to get off, so I handed the rod to Steve who was in the front of the boat, and pulled for a break. Steve switched the anti-reverse on and wound down until the line parted. I never fish with the anti-reverse on as I always back-wind when playing fish. Steve handed me back the rod and I tied on another trace, clipped on a ABU Koster and cast out.

Half a dozen casts later I was just going through the motions, when right out of the blue with the lure only 10 feet under the boat the rod was wrenched from my hands, bouncing along the gunwhale and about to go over the side. The rod was right over and going down into the water as I frantically tried to release the anti-reverse, but it was too late the fish was free. Steve had tightened everything down when pulling for the break, and I hadn't re-adjusted the reel, a good chance and I had blown it.

September and Steve and I were on a small club lake near Asheldam, Essex, landing pike to 18lbs.

I was also spending a fair bit of time bait fishing, stocking up my tanks for the winter months to come. October came and we were heading for Wales again for another blank two days on Llandegfedd. Oh to be able to troll a couple of big livebaits, but it wasn't to be. All the fish came out on the first day yet again. Steve and I decided we will not go again unless we can fish the first day, having only been able to book dates after the reservoir had already been open for days. November came and I had my first trip on Ardleigh in the 1991-92 season, fishing hard for only one run resulting in a fish of 16lbs. On my second session my luck changed with fish of 20¼ lbs and 15lbs, one down only nine to go. Things really started to look up when on my next trip, Tony, Steve and I had stopped to fish Ardleigh on our way up to John Watsons. We had planned to fish Ardleigh, then stop over at John's, fishing Filby Broad in Norfolk the following day. At Ardleigh using drifters I fished my baits right alongside the trout cages taking a nice brace weighing 24½ lbs and 22lbs. Later that evening arriving at John's we all departed for his local to celebrate my brace of twenties, then it was back to John's for a lovely meal washed down with some of his home made wine. The night was finally rounded off with a scotch or two before we tucked ourselves up in bed. Early next morning Steve's shaking me. "Get up Bill its five o'clock".

"Get up, what's he mean get up all I want to do is die". I'd got the mother and father of all hangovers!

Dragging myself out of bed, I finally got dressed and made my way down to the car. Sitting in the back was this horrible thing, it was Tony also looking terrible (mind you he doesn't look much better on a good day). Seeing Tony also in a sorry state, it made me feel a bit better as Steve pulled away from John's. That is until Tony decided he needed a full English breakfast. Pulling up at a cafe opposite the broad, three large breakfasts were ordered but just the smell had me racing for the toilets. Returning after emptying my stomach my breakfast had been finished off by Steve and Tony, not that I had an appetite anyway. At Filby broad we checked out the boats we had booked for the day, and started to load them with our gear. Steve was off for the far distant reed beds at 90 miles an hour, Tony looked at the water then turned a funny shade of green and decided to go back to the car for a lay down. I slowly paddled out 50 yards from the landing stage and dropped the mudweight.

There was a slight breeze blowing across the broad but where I was anchored it was almost a flat calm, although my stomach was telling me it was a force nine gale. "Get your act together Bill", I tell myself, "you're here to catch fish", as I cast two baits off the back of the boat. I then bury my throbbing head into my hands, but five minutes later, parting two fingers I peep out. One of my floats, just five yards off the boat lifted then started to run across the surface disappearing as it went. A run, the way I felt it was the last thing I wanted as I wound down and pulled into the fish. A jack weighing about 3lbs so I slipped my fingers under the pike's chin and leaned over to unhook it. As I looked down the fishes throat I'm ashamed to say I emptied my stomach for the second time, giving the pike an unexpected meal! From the high of yesterday this was certainly the low. "Never again", I tell myself as I row to the bank to take over from Tony in the car. Four days later and back at Ardleigh I was having a fabulous day landing seven pike, five going into double figures with two again breaking 20lbs. Two braces of twenty pounders in a week, somebody up there likes me. Five twenties and I was halfway there.

Steve also gets his tally underway that day; taking a good fish of 24½ lbs. December, and Steve and I are crossing the river into Kent to fish two days on Bough Beech. The first morning was spent trolling big live trout around the reservoir as we map out the water with our echo sounder. We found a good drop-off opposite the landing stage and it was full of bait fish. We made another pass and Steve had a take but pulls out. We decided to drop anchor and fish the drop off for an hour while we eat lunch. The hour passed uneventful, so pulling up the anchor we went off to troll over the feature a couple of times. Perhaps we can induce another run? As we swing round another boat passed through the area and as their floats reached the very spot where we had been sitting, one goes. Five minutes later they are weighing a thirty. I turn to Steve "There's no justice mate".

Day two. I had four takes and pulled out of two good fish, losing one after it had been on for several minutes right alongside the boat. The fish I landed weighed 10½ lbs. There were some massive fish caught that year at Bough Beech to a weight of over 40lbs.

For my next two trips I was drawn back to Ardleigh taking 12 fish up to 19½ lbs. Making 6 more doubles off my total; the reservoir was fishing its head off. Then, in mid-December the weather unfortunately made a turn for the worse, the temperature dropped drastically and the reservoir iced over. Four days later with a big wind blowing, Tony and I took a ride to Ardleigh to see if it was fishable. The wind had broken up the ice but with the big white horses racing across the reservoir it was far too dangerous for boat fishing. We were not geared up for bank fishing, so we went home. Five days later I was back again with Steve. It was Christmas Eve, and I had a brilliant day trolling big baits.

Christmas had certainly come a day early for me, as I landed fish of 17, 19 and a whopping 30½ lbs. Steve also got in on the act with pike to 23lbs. I must fish more Christmas Eves, wasn't it twenty odd years ago I'd had that fabulous day on the 'Big Pond'? I managed to squeeze three more trips on the water before the end of December, taking another 13 doubles, three of them going over twenty pounds. I had also landed my third brace of twenties of the season. If somebody had asked me to walk on water at the time I'd have thought it a doddle! With still ten weeks of the season to go, I had landed nine twenties to date, just one more to go to my target. With the bit between my teeth it didn't take me long to reach my goal, catching it just two trips later in a bag of five doubles.

What a season, but it was to get even better in the weeks to follow. January the 13th, unlucky for some, but not for me. I had an unbelievable day.

Steve and I started by trolling the main body of the reservoir while Bernard made his way down the west arm. Just off the deep water I had a screaming take which resulted in a fish of 22½ lbs. Two small fish later we are trolling over the same area where I had taken the 22½ lbs when one of my baitrunners started to sing. Pulling into the fish it stayed deep hugging the bottom, but finally the pressure told and she broke surface ten yards off the boat. "Blimey it's a lump Steve", I say as my legs turn to jelly: she was just hanging there as I slowly pulled her to the waiting net. As she came ever closer I noticed her gills are starting to flare, "Please don't shake your head", I plead as Steve slipped her into the net and with relief showing on my face. We leave the pike in the net as we drifted the few yards to the bank to do the weighing and photos. 31½ lbs and a new personal best. We concentrated our fishing for the next three hours around the area where I had my fish, but apart from a small double we had no more big fish. Just after midday Steve had to leave for work so dropping him off on the bank I headed up the west arm to see how Bernard had fared.

I had told Bernard to give the bay a seeing to as I felt there could be a good fish or two laying up there. Arriving at the bay, Bernard was anchored just off it. I entered the bay trolling my floats behind me, and they were nicely spread. "How's it going Bern", I shouted across, "Two doubles and a big fish come off, had any more up there Dad?" he asked. "Just one more double before Steve had to leave for work", I answered. Out of the corner of my eye, I notice one of the floats was cutting fast across to the bank. Quickly winding in the other rod I struck into the fish. The rod slammed down and pulled the boat round; three more times the boat circled before I had the fish on the top. Finally, I had her in the net - another good fish. On the bank the needle pulls 28½ lbs.

Ten minutes later, would you believe I was playing yet another big fish.

My first Ardleigh thirty. The blood's mine. 30¹⁄² pounds.

37¹⁄² inches. 24¹⁄² pounds.

I had it close to the boat a couple of times and it looked as big if not bigger than the thirty I had caught earlier that day. Suddenly I felt a ping as a hook pulled out, one more lunge and the pike was gone. Looking back on that day I could have finished up with a brace of thirties and twenties, but it was not to be. Having landed a personal best and two other good fish that day I wasn't that disappointed about the one I lost, well not too much anyway.

Late January, and after taking yet another twenty and several big doubles the reservoir froze over again. To say I was frustrated was an understatement!

Tony, Steve and I tried to launch a boat onto the reservoir to see if we could break the ice, but it was far too thick so we gave up and headed for home. On the 28th I returned with Bernard. The west arm was still frozen over although there was some free water in the main body of the reservoir up to the north arm trout cages.

I plotted up by the valve tower and had just one run which resulted in a fish of $10\frac{1}{4}$ lbs. Bernard stuck it out alongside the trout cages down the north arm taking a nice fish of $22\frac{1}{2}$ lbs. We were well pleased with our catches in the bad conditions.

At the beginning of February I used up the last of my holiday entitlement fishing for three days in the first eight. I had yet another two twenties in bags of four and five doubles. Then, in the second half of February the reservoir finally slows down as the pike head for the shallows with other things on their minds.

With the pike making their way to the spawning grounds the fishing on the reservoir came to an end. So with two weeks of the season left I had a day with Colin and Steve fishing the North Drain in Lincolnshire. We took about 25 small fish, Colin catching the best weighing 14lbs. My last day found me driving to Bough Beech with the trees bent right over in the strong wind. On arriving at the reservoir we were to be disappointed. Ken Crow called the fishing off in the worsening conditions so on the way back home we decided to drop in on Tesco's to see our last hours out.

After a couple of aborted runs my season ended with a fish of 8lbs. At the beginning of the season when I set the target for Steve and I, never in a thousand years did I believe we would have caught the amount of fish we had. Although fishing hard and long, I enjoyed every minute of it, the blank days as well as the good. It's been many years since I've put that much effort into a season. Steve achieved his goal with precisely ten twenties topped by a magnificent pike of 32lbs, just missing out with the doubles though with 49.

My final tally being an incredible 81 doubles, 16 twenties and 2 thirties.

The 1992-93 season started with Steve and I fishing the 'Big Pond' for a couple of hours in the evening; it was my first trip back after a break of 15 years. I landed a 14 pounder, Steve one of 18lbs. The next two weeks I spent some time at Abberton fishing one rod with deadbaits, the other casting out plugs and spinner baits practising for our trip to Llandegfedd in September. "I'm going to catch in that bloody Welsh water if it's the last thing I do". The spinner baits had been made up specially for Llandegfedd and my friend, Jason Davis, had posted them to me from Norfolk. They certainly looked good as I worked them along the banks of Abberton though they didn't catch anything they did look the business. Changing over to a plug I did catch a 10lb and 11½ lbs pike. Perhaps the spinner baits will catch in the deeper water in Wales? September arrived and I head for Llandegfedd, stopping at the Nags Head in Usk for two days. That first morning with the boat loaded up we were waiting for the off while the ranger filled us in on safety and the rules of the reservoir. Then, as the seconds ticked away we were all jockeying for position as we wait for the signal to go. It was just like a grand prix race, everybody trying to reach the north bank first.

On that particular morning Neville Fickling was trying it on. He had unhooked his rope and using an oar was working his way up to the end of the landing stage. I turned to Steve who was on the outboard motor. "If you let Neville beat us out that's your lot", I tell Steve winding him up. Steve grits his teeth, as he hovers over the outboard a look of blind determination comes into his eyes. "Go" shouts the ranger and two dozen outboard motors roar into life. Steve was at full throttle as he spins the boat away from the jetty missing the first three boats by inches. The fourth takes evasive action only to ram boat five. We are really travelling now and Steve is still not looking where he is going as boat six starts to cross our bow. It was Jim Housden and his son and I can see the whites of their eyes, the colour draining from their faces which are a picture of sheer terror. "Steve", I scream as we hit them broadside. Mounting them we nearly go right over the top of their boat. The red slowly leaves Steve's eyes as I apologise and we meekly make our way out of the chaos we had caused. I wouldn't have been at all surprised to have learned one or two anglers had packed up boat fishing after that mad rush of blood by Steve that day. Mind you I suppose that's one way to secure the hotspot, sink half the competition as you pull out!

How did the fishing go? Well, there were three thirties and ten twenties caught that day, all coming out in a tight 40 yard area off the north bank. Where were we then? Bloody-well anchored about 100 yards away, that's where! Although I did catch my first Llandegfedd pike that day taking it on one of the spinner baits and weighing 12lbs. Not much for six days fishing on the reservoir so far.

October, and I took a break from the trout reservoirs heading for Lincolnshire to fish a complex of gravel pits before I'm back in Kent at the end of the month fishing Bough Beech. The complex is made up of three lakes crystal clear and full of weed. Steve and I gave all three a try one after the other taking pike from all of them. Fishing pit one first, which is the biggest, we had a couple of jacks on our second trip. Pit two again we land only small fish and I started to wonder if the 120 mile journey is worth the effort. Towards the end of the day Steve caught an 11 pounder, giving us some encouragement to carry on.

I'm very glad it did, the following week we were on pit three. On the trip before I'd had a quick reconnoitre of the lake. Walking around it I had found a lot of bait fish topping at one end where the pit narrowed. This is the area of the lake I decide to concentrate on. Setting up just as the dawn came, bait fish were hitting the surface everywhere as I dropped out a pumped up roach.

Making up my bait catching rod I soon had a dozen small roach and rudd in the net. Hooking one of the rudd on a paternoster rig I cast my second rod out to where the bait fish were topping most.

Within minutes the paternoster rod was away and I was playing my first double of the day. Quickly unhooking it I re-baited with another rudd and dropped it back in the swim. As I clip on the backbiter the alarm on the pumped up roach signals a run, the culprit being a small pike. Steve was also into a fish. Then, as the morning got lighter and a fair number of fish had been caught, the feeding spell came to an end. Picking up my bait rod again I fished for the roach and rudd, topping up our baits. I must admit I do enjoy a bit of bait-fishing, catching the odd bonus tench, a big roach or rudd, taking me back to my match fishing days. This has to be one of the most enjoyable ways to pike fish, being able to bait fish while piking.

An hour later I had to disregard my bait rod as the pike came back on. The paternoster rod was away again, striking, the rod went right over as the fish was taking line. "This one feels a bit special Steve", I shout. Steve walks up to do the honours, putting a lot of pressure on the fish I soon roll her into the landing net. She certainly was special, weighing 22½ lbs it was one beautifully marked pike. As the day drew to a close I had several more fish and another nice double of 15½ lbs. Two days later, I have a day at Abberton. I wanted to see how the water was fishing as the level was way down. Normally in October it goes really well with a chance of a good fish or two, but with no bait in the culvert I struggled. Fishing all day I had just one run landing a fish of 12lbs saving me having a blank. Two other fish were caught, both small and not much for eight anglers fishing hard. So I was looking forward to going back to Lincolnshire at the weekend. Again, I set my stall at the end of the lake where I had the good bag of fish the week before. Arriving in the half light bait fish were topping everywhere again and I couldn't get my baits out quick enough. Catching some good rudd to over a pound on the bait rod my confidence was soaring, there just had to be one or two big pike in the area. But I was to be disappointed and apart from two missed runs I blanked. Oh well, you can't win them all. Back at Bough Beech, Ken Crow had let us have first crack on the water because we were blown off in March. I wonder? Will it fish as good as it did when it opened for the first time? I'm biting at the bit to fish my allotted two days. Arriving at the reservoir the level was ten feet down and coloured. Trolling every inch of water with our baits (apart from the bird sanctuary which is out of bounds) we didn't get a run. At the end of the day as we unload the boat we are told there had only been two small doubles caught. The weather forecast for the next day was rain and yet more rain.

Loading up the car I put a brolly in, picking up Steve on our way back into Kent for the second day on the reservoir. The weatherman had got it right for once, the rain is hammering down. We trolled for an hour with no success so we decided our best bet was to anchor up and fish the baits hard on the bottom in the coloured water. Sitting there working our baits the rain started to come down even heavier, although we were well waterproofed it was finally getting through. So I put up the brolly, wedging it between Steve and I. Alright so we looked like a couple of wallies with a brolly in the boat but we were dry. Mind you, I wouldn't recommend it with any kind of wind blowing and we were also getting some funny looks from the more macho pikemen. Two hours later the rain hadn't eased at all, in fact it was now coming down by the bucket load. I also noticed the macho pikers had succumbed to the worsening conditions, packing up and going home leaving us two wimps to carry on fishing the reservoir.

At long last one of my floats disappeared, the line was pouring off the

22¹ᐟ² pound pit fish.

Steve with a twenty on the troll.

January 13th - unlucky for some but not for me, as I have an unbelievable day taking fish of 22$^{1/2}$lb, 28$^{1/2}$lb and this magnificent pike of 31$^{1/2}$lb.

What a prat in the hat.

Steve with a 31$^{1/2}$ pounder.

spool and as I wound down my mind went back to last season's big fish catches on the reservoir. I strike, and although fighting well I could tell it was no monster as Steve slips the net under a plump 14¼ pounder. I believe the 14 was to be the biggest caught over the two days. The fishing on the reservoir had certainly slowed down, with hardly any big fish coming out in the months that followed. Some anglers were starting to question the future of the water. I was really hoping the reservoir would pick up, Ken Crow, who runs the fishing on the water deserves to succeed. He has bent over backwards to help us catch fish, supplying trout even netting some roach and bream for us to try. My personal belief is that the trout water pike are short lived fish, packing on weight very quickly, they peak then die. Also I don't think they are as hardy as their non-trout water brothers, stressing up a lot more on being captured. If a trout water has a policy of removing all the small pike and are successful, I believe as the big fish die, with hardly any small fish coming through to take their place it might take several years before one or two make it again.

BEWL BRIDGE RESERVOIR

This picturesque trout reservoir near Lamberhurst in Kent, comprises 770 acres with a depth of 80 feet by the dam wall when full. First opened for pike fishing I believe, around 1978-79, I'd also been told that in the early '80's a number of forty pound plus fish had been netted from the reservoir. It was also rumoured, around that time every year a fish in excess of the British record would turn up in the nets. If there is any truth in the stories surely with that kind of pedigree Bewl Water, if properly managed, would give us some of the best pike fishing in the country. Perhaps our only chance in future would be if the popularity of the trout fishing on the reservoir starts to drop off. The management then might open the water in the winter for pike fishing, to make up the lost revenue making the trout and pike fishing a joint venture. I first fished Bewl with Steve in 1993, and I've had one day there every year since. I enjoy my day there, but one day is enough with the present fishing restrictions, (only large sea deadbaits and lures over 5 inches) and I hate being restricted in my fishing. With a nine o'clock start, and a four o'clock finish, it's what you would probably call a gentleman's day pike fishing. It opens for piking for only eight days a year, three weekends and a couple of days in the week using 30 boats, and since pike fishing has been allowed on the reservoir for those few days a year there have been about six thirties caught on rod and line.

All the fish caught are picked up by the rangers touring round in a boat with a large tank aboard, after which they are then transferred to Ardingly and Tanyard at this moment in time. If the fish were killed I wouldn't fish there (I believe the reservoir is still being netted every year). Turning up that first year there were about 60 anglers assembled on the bank, and what a motley crew they were! Looking at some of the rods the anglers had made up and were holding, my ancient gear looked quite modern. There were fly rods, splitcane rods of all sizes, beach casters, and sea boat rods.

On the few occasions I've fished Bewl I have probably only seen half a dozen ardent pike anglers fishing it. The rest are out for a fun day, and good luck to them. My best day's fishing on the reservoir I shared a catch of nine doubles with lots of small fish, Steve taking the majority of them. That day I also caught two five pound plus rainbow trout both greedily taking very big deadbaits. With 770 acres of water to explore it has many features, a very interesting and enjoyable water to fish.

November 92, I'm back at Ardleigh for my first trip on the water in the new season, but only landing a scraper double and pulling out of another. Steve also caught just one small fish, the few runs we did have coming from the west arm. Checking my diary it seems the reservoir is fishing as slow as it did this time last year. Although at the time there were some rumours going round that most of the pike had died.

Talking to a couple of lads who had fished Ardleigh in the summer they told me they had seen hundreds of dead fish floating around the margins of the reservoir, all big doubles and twenties. Catching only a small jack on my second session on the reservoir I was starting to believe the rumours. I had another day on Bough Beech but the water was just not fishing, with just a few small doubles coming out. I finished my day there with a 12¾ pounder. The following week found Steve, Tony and I travelling to Northampton to fish Pitsford reservoir, a trout water that had also opened for a limited period of pike fishing. Trolling a big deadbait 25ft down in 41ft of water I had a screaming run that turned out to be a big brown trout. My next trip I stayed in Essex fishing at Abberton, giving the trout waters a miss. I want to catch some fish with teeth, not spots. Mind you the way the pike fishing's going I'd probably be better off fishing for trout. Arriving at Abberton the 'big half' is taken so I set up on the natural side left of the culvert. Using my model boat I placed the baits in the bed of an old stream 80 yards away.

Catching fish from the off I had them on paternoster and ledgered dead and livebaits. Nothing big but plenty of pike to 12 pounds. This is more like it and I'm starting to really enjoy myself. That is, before the cormorants moved in! The line was a blur leaving the spool as the first bird picks up the bait 80 yards away. I was quite excited for a minute or two believing I was into a good fish, only to be disappointed as the cormorant surfaced near the bank. Releasing the bird I run out another bait. Forty minutes later I was into my second cormorant, this one tried to take off a couple of times, but finally it was close enough for Steve to grab. The trace and hooks are wrapped around the birds legs so avoiding the sharp beak I took hold of the cormorant while Steve untangled the line. "Right, it's free", shouted Steve. Releasing my grip on the bird it took to the air only for the hooks to pull into my hand. I must admit I'm a bit of a coward when it comes to taking out hooks, even from other people, let alone when it's me. I think it goes back to when I had all those trebles in my head when I was a kid. Steve came to my rescue just ripping the hooks out with his forceps!

December, and I'm back at Ardleigh having six runs in the morning without landing a fish. The pike were just playing with the baits grabbing them then letting go, just like a cat with a mouse. Three of the baits were nearly bitten in half without the floats registering a run. Then, in the late afternoon by the white farm on the west arm I finally set the hooks into a fish. Slipping the net under what I thought to be a good double, I swing it aboard but can't believe how fat the fish is, laying there it looked more like a carp than a pike. Taking out the hooks, I weighed her right away at 24½ lbs. I couldn't believe what I was seeing, three more times I checked the scales. At 37½ inches long with a 22½ girth that runs the length of the body it was the fattest fish for length I'd caught to date. For the rest of the 92-93 season I tried to have at least one day on Ardleigh each week. Nine days in all I landed another 24 doubles and 5 twenties, with the best of the lot weighing 27¼ lbs. So much for all the rumours of dead pike. I was averaging three doubles a trip with a good chance of a twenty. That will do for me!

1993-94 SEASON

Blimey, where has the last 50 years gone, there can't be much time left for this old wrinkly! Anyway my season starts like all the rest stalking carp and catching tench. Then in August Sheila and I have a week's holiday on the River Avon. I wanted to check the river out for piking later in the year.

What a fabulous week's fishing it turned out to be. Fishing only in the mornings or evenings for a few hours (the days spent on the beach) we target the barbel catching one on our second cast. It seemed every time I left Sheila for a minute or two, when I returned she would be into a barbel. Not landing too many but hooking plenty of them nevertheless.

What with the barbel, five pound plus chub, good bream and eels, checking out the pike fishing had taken a back seat. Over the week I probably only pike fished for an hour in all, mind you on most of the Avon you're not allowed to fish for pike until November. Whenever Sheila or I caught a small dace or roach, which wasn't very often, I would put it on my pike rod. Dropping it in a slack or behind a weedbed within seconds it would be taken. Most of the pike being small with just a couple of doubles to 14lbs. Then, towards the end of the week I dropped a small dace behind a large weedbed, the bait had just hit bottom when it was engulfed. The rod went over and the line started to sing as I found myself playing a good fish. In the clear water I could see the pike as it slowly swam just under the rod top, the single hook and piece of poly is clearly visible nicked in the scissors. The fish looks every inch a twenty and as it was lightly hooked I decided not to hand it out, calling to Sheila for the net. Too late, the pike shook it's head throwing the hook. "Quick Min catch me another bait". That's easier said than done. After about an hour using the float rod we'd caught roach to over a pound, a perch nearer two, and a big chub. All miles too big for my single hook rig. Putting three bronze maggots on the ledger rod I cast to a fast glide on the far bank hoping for a dace. Thrusting the rod into Sheila's hand, I told her to hit every knock. The rod tapped Sheila struck and yet another barbel shot off down stream. Finally though, she caught a small roach. Quickly I nick it on the hook and drop it behind the big weedbed and, placing the rod high in the rests I turned on the bait runner. Min makes her way back to her swim in the weirpool, thirty yards further along the bank Watching my line where it enters the water I'm in another world. "Bill, Bill", Min screams bringing me back to earth. Jumping up I can see her rod was right over; yes another barbel cutting fast across the weir, "Give line, give some bloody line", I shout back. Picking up the landing net, I run along the bank but on reaching her the rod sprung back and the fish is off. "Christ Min how many times have I got to tell you to backwind when a good fish runs", I preach to her. Dejected Min cast out another bait. Returning to my swim I'm just in time as my rod top dips violently as the bait runner starts to whine. Striking, the fish surges down stream catching me unaware's the power was unbelievable; this is one lump of a pike. Keeping the pressure on I followed stumbling as I went. There was an angler in mid-river wading out to fish for the barbel. The pike is heading straight for him! What a foolish decision I made, clamping down I try to turn the pike. The rod goes round to its very limit lifting the fish to the surface followed by two enormous swirls the ripples of which reach both banks. The fish dives smacking the water hard with its tail, ripping the hook out as it did so. Hearing the commotion our barbel angler nearly falls over with fright. "Give line, give line", it's Min she's tried to get the action on video. "Give line, give line" she shouts again jumping up and down laughing. "You're not so bloody hot either", she tells me. Oh well, I suppose I deserved that. Looking back I should have spent a lot more time helping Sheila, instead of fishing myself. The trouble was it's been a long time since I've fished a good river like the Avon and on tasting it I couldn't get enough, but I'll be back.

Checking my angling diary for 1993-94, during September and October I was fishing all my local lakes, reservoirs and gravel pits. Having a couple of nice twenties from two of them. I'd even been back to the Lea valley. Mind you I'm only filling in time waiting for the end of the trout fishing on Ardleigh in November. On the last day of October I just couldn't wait any longer, so I arranged a trip to Ardleigh with Bernard, Steve and Tony. Sharing a boat with Bernard we are going to test his new electronic trolling motor. We gave it a very good test trolling all day and the Minn-Kota performs well. How did the fishing go? Just three fish between us, Steve and I had a mid-double, Tony topping us with a twenty. For my first November trip, I had half a day on Abberton with Steve, catching three pike to 15lbs. I'm off to Ardleigh tomorrow so we don't leave it late.

Arriving at the reservoir at 7.00 am, I pick up the permits while Steve loads up the boat. The temperature is in the fifties with not a breath of wind as we push away from the bank. Four baits were quietly lowered into the depths, floats set, rods into the boat rod rests. We started by trolling slowly down the margins of the reservoir, in the stillness there's a magical feel to the air. It's a day for dreams to be made, and made they were.

About 45 minutes passed, and for every one of them we were expecting a run. With the flat calm conditions trolling was easy, in fact the morning was perfect. The floats registering every little movement of the baits. Suddenly one of the bait runners burst into song - my outside rod. The line was leaving the spool fast; I opened the pick up as Steve cut the electric motor, quickly we wind up the other rods. Pulling into the fish a good fighting curve was set in my rod, and by keeping the pressure on I was actually drawing the boat to the pike. We were then right on top of the fish though up to now she hadn't done anything at all just laying there on the bottom. Slowly I pumped the pike up from the depths and she came into view "Look at the width across the back Steve", I croak as the pike surfaced along the side of the boat. Steve manoeuvred her into the net and it was all over in one minute flat. (Mind you let's be honest we really don't want the big ones to fight anyway do we!) Peering in the landing net, laying inside was the biggest pike I'd caught to date. I slumped down on the boat seat completely gob-smacked. On the bank Steve weighed her, I couldn't look. "34lbs". "What". We check again together, yes 34lbs Steve was right. "Oh thank you Lord". For the next couple of days I was walking about like a headless chicken.

In my early years boat fishing I would have to use the oars to troll before we started to use electric motors. The golden rule was to be as quiet as possible even more so when working through very shallow water. The rule holds good inside the boat too, dropping a flask, banging the boat with the rods, clattering inside a tackle box you frighten every pike for miles. As for disturbing the water outside the boat, that's another matter. Over the years I've found it pays you sometimes to actually cause a disturbance on the surface with the oars, even in the shallowest of swims. Noisily putting big boils and swirls on the surface of the water you can sometimes get lethargic pike feeding, attracted to the commotion and on seeing the bait they may strike. For example, the amount of times I've been caught out when being blown into a snag or into the bank. Winding the baits up alongside the boat you then row like mad, then suddenly one of the rods nearly goes over the side as a pike is drawn to the baits. Nowadays, I try to remember always to put my baitrunners back on whenever I've wound the baits in. Then there is the time when you've trolled through a hotspot as quietly as you can without a response; impatiently you swing the boat round to go through yet again and as the floats reach the big disturbance created one stabs down.

Talking about being caught out, I can remember really blowing it at Ardleigh one day in the 93-94 season. Fishing hard all day for very little I had covered all my hotspots landing just one small fish of 7lbs. I decided to finish the day out in the bay down the west arm of the reservoir. Four times I'd quietly trolled through the bay, altering depths of the floats after every

It's a day for dreams to be made, and made they were. The 34 in all it's glory.

troll without a sniff of a fish and as the light starts to go I badly wanted to catch. Right, this calls for drastic action! The wind had freshened now and coming from the south west it was blowing right into the bay as I started my fifth troll. Zig-zagging the boat through the swim parting the water with the oars in a big way, I created boils everywhere. The floats reached a bush five feet from the bank when a fish weighing about 10lbs struck at one of them. As it was only the second fish I'd seen all day, I wanted it. Setting all three floats at six feet I splashed my way round for a second pass by the bush. Again the baits are only feet from the bank when one of the floats disappeared. Releasing the oars I wound up the other rods but as I did so the wind blew me into the bank. Striking, the rod tapped a couple of times as I made contact with the fish, still believing it was the fish that had a go at my floats. I started to use the pike as a lever to pull myself away from the bank. Suddenly the rod went over and kept going right down into the water. "Damn, snagged on the bottom", I tell myself. Exerting a lot of pressure the bottom started to move towards the surface. Believing I was lifting some sort of snag, I was to be completely flabbergasted when a big thirty popped up under the rod top alongside the boat. My legs went as I reached round for the landing net. Christ it was all caught up in some brambles hanging down from the bank! As I tried to free the net the pike started to slowly sink back down tail first, the rod still holding the pike's head up on the surface. Frantically pulling at the brambles only being able to use one hand I was not having much joy though. Guess who's panicking like mad now? The pike was vertically hanging off the rod top not knowing she was hooked. Opening her massive jaws she just spat the bait right back at me. The last thing I remember seeing was her cold eye staring at me as she disappeared into the murky water leaving me as sick as a parrot. But, as luck would have it, not for long. In the run up to Christmas, the fishing had been quite patchy with just a few doubles from Abberton and Lincolnshire, my local gravel pits coughing up only one or two jacks. Even Ardleigh had been fishing slow. I'd managed only one fish over twenty pounds in four trips up to the end of December, although Steve had come good with a pike of 25lbs at the Towers on the 29th. New Year's Eve and I found myself the only boat out, and apart from two bank anglers down the west arm the reservoir was deserted. The weather wasn't bad, the sun was starting to show itself with the temperature in the high forties. The wind was perhaps a little strong for trolling but not impossible. Mind you, catching the 34 in November, I felt any other big fish from the reservoir this year would be a bonus. I made a start plotting up in the deep water but after two hours without a run a move was called for. Up-anchoring I moved over to the south bank where the wind was coming from, so giving me some protection. On the sheltered bank it was a lot more comfortable as I trolled down to the white farm and on reaching the farm, opposite the bay I had my first run of the day. A brief struggle followed a few minutes later my returning a nice pike weighing 18½ lbs. The further I went down the west arm the calmer it became with all the trees shielding me from the wind. Trolling to the very end of the reservoir I had no more takers, but working my way back I missed a run in ten feet of water. I spent some time covering the spot where the pike had taken but couldn't interest it again. Moving on I decided to troll back to the car and call it a day. Being New Year's Eve I didn't want to be late home. Fishing to just past the white farm was uneventful. Passing the west arm car park, I noticed the two anglers on the bank were also packing up. "Another 15 minutes and I'll be packing up also", I think to myself, as I concentrate back on the floats. "Blimey the right one's gone". I cut the motor and wind the other two rods in fast. I'm glad I did because on striking the pike took off like a bat out of hell. It actually towed me for about thirty yards along the reservoir. As the fight went on closer to the boat she continually dived under it and if I'd had an anchor down I would have surely lost her. Eventually, she was on the surface but wouldn't go into the net. Every time I had her over the top and went to lift she paddled out. At long last after a lot of praying and pleading I juggled her in. Letting out a big sigh I drew the net and pike to the side of the boat. It was a thirty but how big? Getting out the weighing and unhooking gear I then lifted her aboard, the hooks easily removed so I lifted her clear of the net, carefully laying her into the weigh sling. Hooking in the Avons and lifting her clear of the boat, the dial spins round, 33¼ lbs. Placing her into a keepsack I motor the few yards to the west arm car park and the two anglers on the bank. Measurements and photos are quickly taken, length 44 inches, girth 24½ inches. A big framed fish I returned her hopefully to get even bigger and to fight another day. What a way to finish the year! I was so high if I hadn't a car I'm sure I could have flown home.

Up to the end of the 1993-94 season several more twenties were to grace my net from Ardleigh. It's the only trout reservoir that keeps producing good pike fishing year after year. The rest seem to have just the one good season, then struggle. With the arrival of the close season Sheila made out a list of all the jobs that need doing, decorating, being at the top of her list. Checking out my paint brushes in the garden shed, they are all as hard as rock, and want replacing.

Before I can get down to my local do-it-yourself I was to be saved by the bell. Dr. James Gardner, Andy Lush and Andy Walker have booked up a week's pike fishing in Ireland, inviting Steve, Bernard and me to go with them. Meeting up at James' parents house in Kent, we transferred our gear into the hired minibus and opening the back doors of the van half of Andy Lush's tackleshop drops out onto the ground! I've never seen so many lures in my life, bloody big boxes of them, but by leaving most of them behind we were then able to squeeze our tackle into the bus.

Twenty-one hours later we arrived at our destination in Co. Galway. Yes 21 hours, blimey you would have thought we had travelled half way round the world instead of just across the sea to Ireland. The weather the previous week had been atrocious, putting the rivers and Irish lochs into the fields. The continuing rain and gale force winds gave us our first mini crisis of the trip. Apart from Andy's lures and a dozen dead roach that I had brought with me, we had no bait. Mind you with the gale force westerly winds still blowing there was no way we would be going out on the big loughs in a boat anyway. The original plan for baits assumed it would be so easy to catch them as needed, after all, this is Ireland, one a chuck or so we were told. All our sea deads would be bought fresh, from the local fishmongers. The only trouble was the rivers were unfishable, the trawlers hadn't been to sea for over a week in the treacherous conditions leaving all the fishmongers fishless. What made it even worse, all the supermarkets in Co. Galway had gutted the few mackerel and herrings they had, making them useless.

James and Andy picked up the several gallons of maggots ordered, asking for information on the best places in the bad conditions where we could possibly use them. There was a small lake connected to the lough, laying in a copse just a few miles from the cottage where we were based. It held bream, roach and some pike, James and Andy were told. So the next day found us all trying to catch some baits from the lake, but apart from James who somehow managed to winkle out a couple of roach we all blanked in the high and coloured, cold water. Towards the end of the day Bernard caught our first pike of the trip, landing a 12 pounder on one of my dead roach. Perhaps I was a little hasty knocking Andy Lush and his lures, Andy being more than justified in bringing half a ton of metal with him. He caught our second pike weighing a mind blowing 2½ lbs on a spinner bait. We are now desperate for bait running about in all directions fishing every little drop of fishable water we could find, but with no success. On the morning of the fourth day of the holiday we headed for Lough Ballycuirke to fish a deep bay where we are told we might stand a chance, as the roach and bream hole up there in the cold weather. As we tackled up on the fishing platforms our luck was about to change when a party of Irish anglers turned up. Informing us they were part of the national match team, and wanted to practice in the bay with all the extra water in the lough the platforms were the place to be. So a deal was struck. If we were prepared to give up the platforms, they would give us any bait caught at the end of their match. Can you believe it, the Irish national team bait fishing for us! If they can't catch us some baits then we are in deep trouble. So, Bernard and Andy Walker dropped back to fish a small lake we had passed. James and Andy Lush go off to check out Lough Corrib, while Steve and I trudge round the other side of the bay keeping an eye on our Irish investment. As the match comes to an end the Irish lads keep their part of the bargain supplying us with 60 roach and bream, giving us about ten baits a man. God bless them.

Day five and the wind had abated somewhat and with some bait at long last but only 2½ days left we were going to hit two loughs to see if we can find fish. James and Andy Lush fished Lough Corrib, Steve, Bernard, Andy Walker and me doing Lough Ballycuirke. Float trolling we found a hot area off a point and alongside a reed bed. Steve started the ball rolling with a 17¼ lbs fish and a short time later I chip in with a 13 pounder. Bernard and Andy are also into fish, Bernard having three doubles in quick succession. Lots of small fish followed, we are having to land up to three fish on the same bait before it disintegrated completely. James and Andy blanked on Corrib with the wind picking up again it was not the place to be. So we all decided with very little time left to go back to Ballycuirke in the morning and fish the productive area we found. A good day at last with us all getting stuck into fish, James having several doubles up to 19½ lbs, Andy landing a couple of good fish, with me finishing the day with a 21¼ pounder. On the last day we had just a few hours fishing before heading off home so we share out the last of the bait. It worked out at one and a bit each! As we loaded the boats and pushed out, the weather was beginning to deteriorate. In fact, it went through the complete spectrum that morning, from brilliant sunshine to snow, hailstones and driving rain. One of the good things to come out of the

Irish trip, Bernard had purchased half a dozen ex-army rubberised ponchos from his local Army and Navy store. Costing only a few pounds they were a loose circular cloak type garment with a hole in the centre for the head to poke through into a hood. For boat fishing in very wet weather I haven't found anything better for keeping you dry. How did our last few hours in Ireland go? Dropping in my last bait it was taken instantly by a hard fighting 15½ pounder. Returning the pike I repositioned the hooks on what was left of the bait, only for it to be taken again by the very same fish 100 yards away, bringing my Irish trip to an end.

Considering we had no bait until the last couple days, the adverse weather conditions, landing 18 good doubles between us wasn't a complete disaster. The Guinness was good, and some of the weird cries Andy Walker made while playing table football in the pub had me in stitches. What did I learn from the trip? Oh yes, make sure in future to bring plenty of bait with me.

1994-95 season. As the close season came to an end, there was a lot of talk that it could possibly be the last one. Abolishing it and having year round fishing may make it a good or bad thing for the angler, I suppose only time will tell. Let's hope the pike stocks don't suffer when they gather in large numbers during their spawning period. Seeing this then could possibly be the last time there is a close season, light-heartedly I decided to try and catch twenty twenties in the 1994-95 season, having come close on one or two occasions in the past. It's probably my last chance of trying to achieve it. I weighed up my chances of success, time on the bank, working full time with Fords so the actual amount of time fishing may not be enough. Venues, if Ardleigh fishes as good as it's done for the last few years, and if my local gravel pits, lakes and reservoirs chip in, no problem. Enjoyment, you've really got to enjoy your fishing and when the weather becomes bad sitting on cold windswept reservoirs blanking week after week it can become more like work than fun. Will my enthusiasm stand the test? Well it hasn't waivered too much in the last 50 years, and I did enjoy fishing hard with Steve a couple of seasons ago. I didn't think it would be a problem. Cost? Well it can't be cheap that's for sure what with bait, transport, boat and day tickets. Social and family life will definitely suffer spending nearly all my free time and energy fishing. Luck, to reach my goal, I'll need more than my fair share. I ask myself, is it all worth the effort? Yes you're a long time dead, let's go for it!

June '94, and it's late afternoon as I started my season off plug fishing a local gravel pit. The temperature was in the high seventies, carp topping everywhere as I worked the plug just under the surface alongside the dense reeds. The rod was wrenched round and the water explodes as a pike left the water like a missile shaking its head violently. You can understand why the lure boys love their summer piking, seeing that big bow wave heading towards you as old esox homes in fast hitting the lure on the surface, it certainly gives you a buzz. The pike dived into a weedbed making a last lunge for freedom frightening a big common carp to jump over my line. Working the pike back through the weed I hand it out, weighing about eight pounds it's had me right over, the way it went I thought I'd hooked something twice the size. Removing the plug and holding the pike by the wrist of the tail upright in the water for a few seconds I gently released her. As it swam away yet another good carp boiled in front of me. With all the carp showing the temptation was too much, so removing the plug I tied on a no.6 hook and catapulted chum mixer out. I had nine months to catch my twenty twenties, plenty of time I kid myself.

With all the hot weather we were having that summer it was nearly six weeks later, the beginning of August before I was finally back piking, concentrating on two lakes for only a couple of hours before having to go to work. I fished small poly'd lives on a big single, and having success in the shape of some nice conditioned doubles. It gave me encouragement and confidence to increase my effort on the waters. That extra effort paying off finally with three good twenties in four mornings. Before August was out I caught another two; carrying on the good work in the first week of September with yet another one making a total of six in 12 days. What a result, six twenties from gravel pits in a fortnight. Towards the end of the second week's fishing I noticed a couple of the doubles were repeat captures. When one of the twenties visited me for a second time, I decided it was time to move on. After all it's only a bit of fun, we don't want to hammer the pike just for the sake of it so I gave the fish a rest and looked elsewhere. My next trip saw me heading for Abberton one sunny September afternoon. I was having to work the mornings being on the early shift that week with Fords, so I was going to have a quick reconnoitre of the reservoir checking out the water level and the thickness of the weed. With the brilliant start I'd made on the pits I was bubbling over with enthusiasm and wanted to keep the ball rolling. There was hardly any pressure on the reservoir until October, and it can fish really well sometimes. It was 4.00 pm as I pulled up outside the gate on the road that runs over the small half of the reservoir. Slipping on my Polaroids to check out the water, slightly down, plenty of weed showing with a touch of algae. Taking the lure rod from the back of the car I had a couple of casts before heading for the big half. In all my years fishing Abberton I've still to catch a twenty from the small end, mind you I haven't done a lot of time there. Meanwhile a coach pulls up and some senior citizens disembark. Milling around the gate they were taking in the scenic view. Clipping on a Big S plug, grabbing the landing net and forceps I go to pass through the gate. "Much in here mate?" one of the pensioners asked. Being up close to them now most of them looked younger than me. "Yeah, there's some half decent fish", I replied. "What are you fishing for?" asks another. "Pike", I tell him. "They're dangerous, got a mouthful of teeth", he turns and tells his friends. "Before taking the hook out do you kill it first?" he enquires. "Christ no the hooks are easily removed I kiss it and return it to fight another day", I reply getting just a little annoyed. "I bet he's been bitten a few times", the pensioner whispers to his mates. My hearing has been bad now for a number of years, but I must have been having a good day and heard him. Holding up my hands "Listen mate, I've caught thousands of pike over the last fifty years and I've still got all my fingers", I brag. "You've caught thousands you say, then there's a good chance we will see you catch one today", he replied winking at his mates. "I don't see why not", I tell him.

"You like to do your fishing in comfort then?", he replied looking down at my feet. I've still got my carpet slippers on. "That's right mate from sitting in front of my fire to a fish on the bank", I answer quick as a flash. The gods must have been looking after me that day, my very first cast the plug was taken. Thank you, thank you. Playing the pike hard I got the fish to tailwalk a couple of times and I'm making sure our older friends on the bank are seeing all the action, well you would wouldn't you! They had all filed through the gate now and are standing behind me shouting encouragement with every movement of the fish. It's close now and the plug was clearly visible hanging from the jaws. "Right I'm going to hand it out and unhook it", I tell my audience. The pike looked about ten pounds, as it touched the concrete slope it thrashed its tail sending a shower of water over my new found friends, making a couple of them jump back a yard or two. Bending down I slip my fingers under the pike's chin lifting it clear of the water. Grasping the treble with the forceps I jerk the plug free. Holding the fish firmly with the mouth open, they all wanted to see the pike's armoury,

Bernard with a 28$^{1/2}$ from Ardleigh.

21$^{1/4}$lb from Lough Ballycuirke.

Bernard with a 30½lbs pike that 2 years later weighed 39½lbs.

Barry Summerhaye with the 39½.

some not too close mind you. "There, that was no trouble was it, I haven't a scratch and the pike's unharmed", I say. They are hanging on my every word now, kissing it on the back of the head I released her to the sound of clapping. Yes half of them were actually clapping. One old dear was sitting on the grass, I believe the excitement was too much for her. Guess who's head had swelled to twice the size, little did I know that within ten minutes it would be deflated to the size of a pea.

Working all the water for thirty yards further along the bank, I had no more strikes. Out of the corner of my eye I noticed the last elderly gentleman boarding the coach. Winding the plug in fast I decided to make a move too, but would you believe it a five pound jack grabs the lure five yards from the bank so clamping down I wound it straight to my feet, turning round I check to see if my friends in the coach had noticed. Unfortunately they had, the coach was pulling away and had stopped behind me. Grinning like a Cheshire cat exchanging thumbs up I felt a sharp pain in my toes, looking down the pike's bitten into my slipper. I tried to prise the fishes jaws open, only to find two of the barbed trebles had also embedded into the slipper. Searching for my forceps I remembered they were laying thirty yards along the bank on top of the net and dying with embarrassment I tried to keep the pike still as it jumped about on the end of my foot. I'm frightened to look up at the coach windows now, as I carefully work my foot out of the slipper. Finally, I managed to get free, half of my beige sock had gone red matching my face. The pike still had a firm hold of my slipper as I carried it to where I left the forceps. Plodding along the bank I slowly turn towards the occupants of the coach and as our eyes meet we all burst out laughing. Those few hours at Abberton certainly brought my feet back down to earth, well one of them anyway. Moving on I had no more twenties in September but plenty of sport with some high doubles. As October approached with the gravel pit pike under my belt I felt extremely confident about reaching my goal. It was the middle of October when I had my first trip of the season to Ardleigh. Sharing a boat with Steve, James Gardner and Andy Lush joined us at the reservoir. What a fantastic red letter day it turned out to be, with the pike mad on the feed. Steve and I had at least thirty takes from all over the reservoir that day. Checking my diary we caught quite a few good doubles topped by a brace of twenties for me weighing in at 23 and 22½ pounds. A 26 pounder for Steve with James getting in on the act with a 23½ pounder. Steve also pulled out of a good fish leaving him a shaking wreck, it certainly was a brilliant day. Ardleigh is one hell of a water. Looking back on October I definitely made a wrong decision which was to cost me dear.

With Ardleigh fishing it's head off I came off the reservoir for a couple of weeks and fished my local gravel pit trying to catch one particular fish with no joy. The way Ardleigh was throwing up her big fish in October I should have stayed on the water capitalising on my earlier success. James had taken up residence on Ardleigh now, taking the reservoir apart with some incredible catches. On my return the weather had become unsettled and it was the first of November before I was back on the winning ways with a scraper twenty. Two weeks and half a dozen trips later I caught my tenth one of the season going 25¼ lbs in a bag of five doubles. Only the middle of November and I'm halfway there. A couple of days later guess what, I'm back at Ardleigh again and do I have a result! The weather was good, light s-w winds, temperature sixty degrees. Making a start trolling the deep water by the dam wall, I had a 15lb straight away, and about an hour later I had a second run in the exact spot where I had the earlier fish. After a spirited fight in the deep water I slipped back a nice plump 18 pounder. Dropping the mud weight I sit on the area for a further hour with no response so I decided to rest it for a while and have a look down the west arm. Slowly trolling from the dam to the 'wire' I had another two chances, pulling out of one after a few seconds which felt small, the other I missed completely. Then by the white farm I took a 17lb, my third double of the day. Releasing her I continued trolling the west arm continually resetting the depths of the floats as needed. I was fishing in five feet of water now as I neared the end of the reservoir. Slowly turning the boat I head back to deeper water and as the floats swing round lifting the baits high in the water one was taken. The rod took on a slight curve, the baitrunner starting to sing as line was stripped from the reel. I didn't bother to wind up the other rods as the fish had pulled well clear of the remaining floats. Striking, the pike took to the air alongside the reeds; weighing about 12lbs, she was to flare her gills at me three more times before I have her safely in the boat. What a spectacular fight the pike gave me in the shallow water, ain't life grand. Continuing back up the reservoir, I reached the wire with no more action coming to the rods. Checking my watch it was 2.00 pm. Eager to get back to the deep water mark where I had caught the fish in the morning I got a strong feeling I might just catch a decent fish there in the last remaining hours. Winding up the rods and removing the baits from the water opening up the Minn-Kota, I powered

Dr. James Gardner was taking the reservoir apart topped with this huge pike weighing 38¹ᐟ²lbs.

27¹ᐟ⁴lb the best of eight doubles.

towards the dam wall. As I pass Tony Corless by the point I asked him how he had done. He informed me that he had caught a mid-double and lost a good fish earlier in the day, coming adrift after several minutes. Commiserating with Tony I then moved on to my deep water swim. Cutting the electric motor I drifted the last few yards and quietly lowered the mud weight. Picking up the first rod, taking out a 3oz lead with an elastic band through it, I hooked in one of the trebles to plumb the depth, setting the stop knot so the bait was a foot off the bottom. Putting on a new lively bait I cast out, then repeated the process with the other rod. With both rods fishing I pour myself a welcome cup of tea, at peace with the world as I reflect on the good sport I've been lucky enough to have had so far that day.

Twenty minutes passed, the baits were working well but had attracted nothing so far, but I was sure there was at least one good fish somewhere down there. Impatiently I baited up one of my trusty old rods that I made up for the King George reservoir 25 years before. Ten feet long with a 2½ foot cork handle, they are ideal for boat fishing if it goes over the side it will float! Setting the depth I dropped the bait tight to the trout cage, the float working right along the net that hangs down the side of the cage. Suddenly the float buried itself and the line was disappearing down into the hole where the float had been a couple of second before. Tightening down to the pike I knew straight away it was a lump with the rod right over and not going anywhere, just sitting there in 30 feet of water. The fish was now under the boat still a long way down, and starting to make for the anchor rope. Locking up I pumped like mad knowing that if it reached it, all would be lost. It was stalemate as I hung on for grim death giving nothing either way when all of a sudden I was putting line back on the reel, she was coming up! Peering down to where the line entered the water, straining my eyes to get a glimpse of the fish and my heart beating like a drum, a large shadow started to appear from the depths. Seconds later a magnificent pike surfaced in front of me; sinking the landing net I drew the fish towards me. She went in first time, thank God, if it hadn't I don't think my old ticker would have taken the pressure. Grasping the net I struggled to lift her into the boat and as I unfolded the mesh the hooks fell out! The moment of truth. With the pike safely in the weigh sling I lifted her clear of the boat; 34¼ pounds. I was speechless. Congratulations came from Tony and James Gardner and transferring the pike and myself to Tony's boat we head for the shore for a quick photo session. Running a tape along her flank she measured 44¼ inches to the fork of the tail. Just one more long, admiring look and off she went, so ending a very special day for me. Would you believe I was back to Ardleigh the next morning, again landing an 18 pounder in the first hour. It was almost dark when I had my second fish, boating a nice 24 pounder along the dam wall. Packing the gear away and into the car I noticed my old rod that had caught the 34¼ yesterday was badly split, in two places, eight inches from the top eye. It seems all the pressure I applied on stopping the pike from reaching the anchor rope was too much for it. Being in constant use for the last 25 years, putting good fish on the bank it had finally worn out, a bit like me I suppose! Sadly, I decided to retire it, the rod having fought its last fight. In December, the weather became very changeable, the temperature was up and down with the wind at gale force at times. Even so I still managed to fish Ardleigh another 6 times that month. Blanking on one of the days, landing 12 pike over the remaining five. Ten being doubles, the best two weighing in at 19 and 21 pounds. The reservoir was definitely slowing down though. At the start of January I caught another Ardleigh twenty, the only run I had all day, but as the reservoir was not fishing, I was well pleased with my fish. Two days later with half a day free before work, I blanked, but the reservoir was colouring up fast with all the rain and water being pumped in. On my next trip Ardleigh was completely full with coloured water. The kiss of death normally but I did have two runs though missed them both. My final day on Ardleigh in January. I had to plot up in the strong winds and driving rain and was lucky to catch a low double in the last knockings.

February came but there was still a lot of colour in the water and again just like the start of last month I have only the one run, which lucky for me turns out to be another twenty. Ten boats were out that day but apart from my fish there was only one other double caught. With the coloured water still in Ardleigh, strong winds, and the reservoir not fishing too well I took a couple of days on Abberton. It made a nice change to be on the bank again after struggling in the boat for weeks in the bad conditions. My first day back on my old haunt, fishing one rod with a polylive, the other working a drifter. And a very enjoyable day it turned out, landing several pike to 11lbs. Three days later I had another half day on the reservoir before work. Again, plenty of runs coming on poly trout and sardine, in fact, it became so hectic I was wet through having to deal with the rods in the torrential rain. Talking to some of the lads on the reservoir I commented on how well Abberton was

44¼ inches to folk of tail - 34¼lbs.

fishing and they informed me the water had fished very well for the last couple of months with some big twenties being caught. It was also rumoured that a thirty had come out two days before, right in the middle of my two visits. Hadn't I told Steve all year that Abberton was due a big fish or two this season? The second half of February with 16 twenties caught and time running out fast I put all my eggs in one basket and returned to Ardleigh for three more sessions. The water was a lot clearer, the temperature had risen to a healthy 52 degrees, although it was still hard fishing in the continuing wet and windy conditions. At the end of the day having five runs, with three pike boated the top fish went 16lbs it looked encouraging. A week later I was trolling through the deep water when the two floats disappeared simultaneously. Striking into the right-hand one first and on feeling the fish I put the rod back into the boat rest, and switched the baitrunner on. I then quickly pulled into the second pike playing it hard to the boat. Leaving it in the landing net I hooked the net over the rowlock and commenced playing the first fish. As the pike surfaced alongside, unhooking the net off the rowlock I managed to scoop it in on top of it's mate. Both pike looked good doubles so I weigh only the slightly bigger one at 18¾ pounds. I've still got a chance, and I won't give up yet at least not until the fat lady sings anyway, (no, I'm not talking about you Min). Although fishing on well into dark I had no more runs that day, it seems I caught the only two feeding fish together.

My last day on the reservoir in February I share a boat with Bernard. The only place we can conjure up a run or two is in the very shallow water, it seems a lot of males have moved onto the spawning areas and are waiting for the big females to arrive. Although we had ten runs most of them dropped off. I believe the males were just jostling for the best positions striking at anything and everything. With only a couple of days left before Ardleigh closed for coarse fishing my only chance now to reach my target was if the females moved onto the shallows soon. If they do move down I'm going to make sure I'll be waiting for them. The 2nd of March and only two weeks left, I had a half day at Abberton with Wayne Sutton. Working my drifter out 150 yards plus, the vane slipped beneath the waves and five minutes later I was weighing a twenty. Number 17 and 22¾ lbs, well pleased. The Abbo pike certainly gave me a boost, setting me up for my final push at Ardleigh the following morning. Loading the boat in record time I didn't bother to troll instead headed straight for the shallows, putting the rods together as I went. With the shallows looming fast the thoughts were flooding through my mind. "Will the big girls be there? if so will they be feeding? will I catch?" Cutting the motor the boat was hardly moving as I entered the shallow water. Dropping two lively baits over the side I let out some line and with the floats now working about 15 yards behind the boat I began the troll along the margins. The temperature was in the low forties and strong winds were still with us. The good news though, it wasn't raining and the sun was trying to break through. As the first rays penetrated, one of my floats disappeared. Winding down I swept the rod back, nothing! "Did I snag the bottom?" Retrieving the float I checked the bait and as my old mate Colin Benbrook would say, "It was well mauled".

We were in business, changing the bait I carried on trolling down the reservoir. An hour passed with no more pike showing interest in the baits. Doubts started to creep in, perhaps the big females still haven't moved to the shallows, should I fish the deep water, my instincts tell me to stay put so I resist the temptation to move and carry on fishing the shallows. Forty minutes later I was to be rewarded with another run, this time I made contact and the fish didn't feel bad. With fingers crossed it might just be a twenty

161

and as it rolled on the surface it certainly looked like one. Drawing the pike toward the landing net I noticed a flying treble, the other was just nicked on the side of the jaw. Being extra careful to make sure the loose treble didn't catch the net as I landed her; lots of pike are lost in these circumstances. So I was relieved to have her safely in the boat and weighed at 22lbs. A couple of quick photos and I was back fishing with increased vigour. Within minutes of resuming I was into another fish, again the pike feels like a good one pulling the boat round as I slacken off for a second and pass the rod under one of the others. On tightening up again the fish was gone, damn it. I made a mental note of the exact spot where I had the run, lining it up with a bush on the bank. Rebaiting I then continued trolling on and off the margins. I note to come back in an hour seeing the pike was only lightly hooked I might be able to persuade it to take again. I'm so wrapped up and concentrating on my fishing that hour had just flown by. The only other action came in the shape of a male fish about seven pounds, which had clamped onto a big bait and I shook it off alongside the boat. Slowly I trolled through the area where I had lost the pike earlier and as the floats reached the spot I had lined up with the bush, I was holding my breath with anticipation. Ten yards further on the floats are still visible, the baits had brought no response. Passing through a second time, as the floats reached the spot I cut the motor and quietly dropped the mud weight. Leaving the baits to fish the area while I pour myself a welcome cup of tea. As I screw the top back on the flask one of the floats started to run towards the bank sinking down as it went. Picking the rod up I could still see the float two feet under the surface, it slowed right down, the pike coming to a stop five yards from the bank. Winding up fast to the float, pulling the rod round, it goes over and stays there. It's always a good sign if the rod doesn't kick, nine times out of ten its a good fish. This one is no exception.

Keeping a tight line on the pike I soon had her in the net, I don't want to make the same mistake twice! Good job I did too, as I swing her aboard I noticed the hooks had fallen out in the net. 21½ lbs my second twenty of the day and my nineteenth of the season, just one to go. Being so close now I was a bit reluctant to lose time in taking her to the bank for a photo, but I'd been recording every twenty caught this year. So after a bit of a disaster with the camera falling over a couple of times, I finally got a shot off. Releasing her in double quick time I pushed away from the bank, there was at least two hours of good fishing time left. The light began to fade when I had a

22³⁄₄lbs from Abberton number 17 only three days to go.

screaming run on the left-hand rod, line was leaving the spool in a blur. Switching the ratchet off I turned the handle and engaged the reel, leaning back into the fish as all hell breaks loose. The pike was still moving at 100 miles an hour down the reservoir and I was having to backwind like mad. Finally the pressure started to tell and the pike was coming back towards the boat. A broad back humps on the surface then dives taking line again. I'm counting chickens when the rod suddenly springs back and the pike is off. All the fish I've had or lost so far have been lightly hooked, feeding it seemed was not number one on their minds. Although I carried on fishing well into dark, no more runs were forthcoming.

The 4th of March, and my last day on Ardleigh. Fishing the reservoir with James Gardner I again head straight for the shallows, while James started off trolling the deep water. I was extremely confident of catching after my brace of twenties from the reservoir yesterday. Nothing could stop me now from reaching my goal, me thinks. As I started the troll in the half light, oh was I to be disappointed. Where the pike were showing some interest in the baits yesterday, they had completely switched off today, and apart from one small pike that dropped off as I lifted it out, I blanked. James had fared no better on the deep water, also losing the one small fish he hooked that day.

The 6th of March and back to Abberton. I had four runs, landed three, one on a drifter two on pumped up eel.

The 11th of March, finished work at 2.00 pm, shot across to Abberton for three hours, had just one chance and missed it.

The 13th of March, unlucky for some, but it was the last chance to catch the twenty I wanted. The plan was to spend the first few hours on a pit, hoping on catching in an area where I'd caught big fish at this time of year before. If after a couple of hours with no success I'll drop back and fish Abberton for the rest of the day. Arriving at the pit in the dark it took two trips to carry all the gear, bait, and model boat to my swim. As dawn came some fish started to show against the rushes 15 yards further along the bank. Casting two baits at the disturbance and clipping in the backbiters I sat back in the bed chair expecting a run any second. Suddenly the rushes in front of me part as some pike come crashing through. There laying before me was a big female with three male escorts by her side. The pike almost beached herself right by my feet it would have been easy for me to bend down and lift her out. Winding in the rods, I decide to come off the pit leaving them to carry on undisturbed. I don't think lifting out a big twenty by the tail

21¹ᐟ²lbs. My nineteenth twenty of the season. Reluctantly I go to the bank for a quick photo. After a disaster with the camera I finally get a shot off.

counts. As I collect the last of my gear the rushes are alive now with dozens of spawning pike.

It was 9.00 when I arrived at Abberton, the big half being taken with rods stretching from corner to corner. Checking the small half there was only Adrian Kisbury fishing the culvert swim on that side of the reservoir. Moving 30 yards to the left of Adrian I boat out two baits 90 yards, dropping them into the old stream bed. Checking the alarms are working and making up the landing net I placed it between the two rods before I walked down to Adrian for a chat. He told me that not much had come out, so far just a couple of small fish to the lads across the road. Never mind, there was plenty of time yet and my best chance will come in the last hour. The 'small half' of the reservoir has always been a good bet for a decent fish as it gets dark. I'm trying to give myself some hope, but deep down I know in my heart I've probably blown it by now. With the passing of every hour I was becoming more resigned to failure. I'd changed one of the rods over to a drifter putting on my biggest livebait, the other a special piece of eel, six inches of head section I've been saving all year. Sitting behind my rods I started to talk to them, willing one of them to register a run but as the day drew to a close, the big side having given up another couple of small fish, with Adrian catching a double on a dead roach in the culvert. Slowly packing away the gear I left the rods fishing right to the last, even packing away the landing net. Doing a silly thing like that would normally produce a run. Suddenly something wet and heavy hits me hard smack on top of my head. Turning round I thought one of the lads across the road had lobbed half a mackerel at me, but there was no one there. Whatever it was it was starting to slide down the back of my neck. Checking it out I was to be rewarded with a handful of green slime, the culprits being a flock of Canada geese coming in to roost on the banks of the reservoir for the night. I believe someone up there was trying to tell me that's my lot, bringing my season and quest to an end, agonisingly just one twenty short.

Looking back on my 1994-95 season I suppose spending a fair bit of time fishing for a big fish at the Warren, (a local gravel pit) no doubt was to cost me my twenty twenties. After saying that, what a brilliant season I'd had catching 19, enjoying every minute spent on the bank. Talking about time spent on the bank, re-reading the last few pages, it probably looked like I was catching a pike nearly every other cast. So let's put it in perspective, and have a look at the facts and figures of the 1994-95 season. Working shifts full time I was able to fish for a few hours in the week, before or after work, some weekends, also a bit of my holiday entitlement. It all works out at 87 visits to the venues, 50 part days and 37 full days. Trying to be selective I fished waters only where I thought I was in with a chance of a twenty. I caught a total of 123 pike which works out at under 1½ fish a session. Of the 123 pike caught, 60 were under ten pounds, 63 being doubles, making it an average of 4½ trips for every twenty landed. What started out as only a bit of fun, I must admit became quite heavy at times, but once again I must say for the best part most enjoyable, I'm glad I tried.

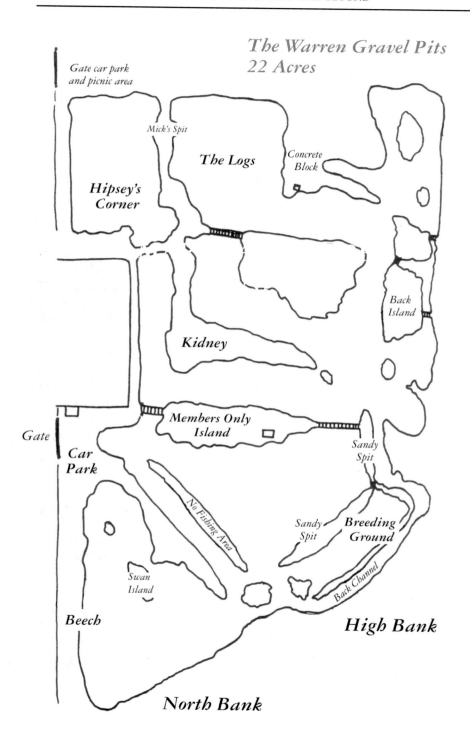

The Warren Gravel Pits
22 Acres

Gate car park
and picnic area

Mick's Spit

The Logs

Concrete
Block

Hipsey's
Corner

Back
Island

Kidney

Members Only
Island

Gate

Sandy
Spit

Car
Park

No Fishing Area

Sandy
Spit

Breeding
Ground

Swan
Island

Back Channel

Beech

High Bank

North Bank

9

THE WARREN MONSTER

I had just finished writing the chapter 'Monsters and Myths' when I found myself holding Britain's first authenticated 50 pound pike. Summing up that chapter I wrote "Do I now believe in Monsters?, Certainly not, well 'er perhaps just a little bit". Am I glad I added that. I was going to re-write it but decided to leave it as it was, and make the 'Warren Monster' my final chapter.

This story started over thirty years ago, way back in 1963 when I first fished the Warren with my old school mate Ray Alexander. Catching the train from East Ham to Stanford-le-Hope, it was a baking hot day as we made our way round the back of the pit. Checking out all the reed fringed bays and channels it was like entering another world. Laying on my stomach peering through the rushes I watched some carp tenting under the duck weed. Slowly parting the weed with my rod I caught sight of a big common, the sun's rays glinting off the big brass scales. We eye each other for a second or two then it slowly drifted away. Needless to say I spent most of the day trying to catch it. Ray was fishing a small bay, stalking a couple of carp that were dibbling amongst the weed by a little island Finally catching one on a piece of crust and weighing 12 pounds, a nice mirror and Ray's first double. With Ray's success that first trip to the new water I remember we spent the rest of the summer fishing the Warren. In the weeks that followed, whenever I was on the lake the time seemed to stop still. I found it a magical place especially when pursuing the big common! One morning I found it grubbing about by some reed stems in 18" of water. It took me 15 minutes to work my way round to it, crawling through brambles and a bed of stinging nettles. The carp was still pre-occupied with its head buried in the silt. Quietly I lowered a lump of crust alongside it. Ten minutes passed and suffering with cramp yet the carp was still digging, so I decide to try and tempt it with a lobworm. Lifting up the crust the hook pulled through leaving it floating on the surface.

Picking out the biggest lobworm I nicked the hook in the head, dropping it down 12 inches from the carp's mouth. The fish buried it's head back down into the silt. The lobworm arched it's back and, just like a mini sea serpent starts bounding along the bottom towards the carp startling the fish as it made contact with the gill plate! Moving off the carp circled round then came back to it's original position, sucking in the loose piece of crust as it did so! Suddenly the carp's pectoral fins were working like mad, it had spotted my lobworm trying to crawl up a reed stem. With my heart in my mouth the carp glided over and sucked it up. Striking, the hook flew out of the water two feet away from the carp. "Damn" the lobworm had escaped from the hook! As the carp bow waved out of the channel I shouted after it "I'll catch you one day". Although I saw it on several further occasions, I never did get the common to take my bait again. When the carp weren't showing Ray and I would do a bit of bream bashing, or fish for the pristine rudd the pit held. As for pike there were none present in the Warren at that time.

It was ten years later, in the early seventies when I returned to the Warren with Tony Strover. With my eel head on I'd heard a whisper of some good eels being caught at the lake. Arriving late afternoon Tony was targeting the carp being completely carp mad, while I concentrated on the eels. Putting out two small deadbaits we were an hour into the session when I had a screaming run. The speed the line was leaving the spool it can only be one thing and sure enough two minutes later I had a 2½ lbs wriggler in the net. As the sun started to disappear below the horizon, I missed another fast run. I was looking forward to the evening fishing when a whistle blew, followed a short time later by the bailiff walking round and telling us to leave the fishery, as only full club members can fish on after dark. Disappointed we leave. Still, and as far as I know there weren't any pike in the Warren at that time.

It wasn't until the end of the '70's, beginning of the '80's that I was back fishing the Warren again, having moved to Pitsea in December 1976. Stanford-le-Hope was only eight miles away, so the Warren became one of my local waters. Popping over the lake for a couple of hours before or after work, two rods were permanently made up ready with just the rest of the bare essentials in a small haversack. Travelling light I would walk round the pit taking carp off the top or catching them on the float when they were bubbling. I would always carry a pack of deadbaits with me, putting two out for the eels when the carp weren't having it. Sometimes, using dead roach and rudd as big as eight inches the baits were catching lots of eels but not once were they taken by pike, I'm so confident there were no pike present. I never did use a wire trace at that time. Wayne Sutton and my son Bernard, were also putting in some time for the eels and we found the majority of the eels weighed between 2 and 3 pounds. Although I heard that eels in excess of 5 pounds had been caught by club members fishing at night, being restricted to the daylight hours we never did top one over 4 pounds. Then in 1983 Bernard caught our first pike from the Warren, landing a 7lb fish that had taken a lobworm on opening day. Having fished the Warren on and off for the last 30 years, it was the first pike I'd seen come from the lake. It turned out not a one off either; on Bernard's very next trip fishing from the back island with half a roach for eels he was bitten off twice. Finally, he managed to land one of the culprits, a 12 pounder. Talking to another angler some time later about Bernard's fish, and the sudden appearance of the predators I remember saying, "I wonder where they had come from?". The angler replied, "The bailiff reckons there's a bloke who drives a yellow escort van with a pike painted on the sides, possibly putting them in". Blimey, that's my van he was talking about, honest hands on heart it wasn't me.

I did hear a rumour when researching this chapter that those first early fish had come from Berwick Pond at Rainham. It was some years later the Lakeside pike were also rumoured to have found their way there. In 1988 the pike were well established in the Warren and Mick Edwards started fishing for them knocking them out like there was no tomorrow. In 1989 Bernard was having a great time catching lots of big doubles from Hipsey's Corner, while I was having some nice doubles from the north bank. The Shell angling club which I believe was run by mainly match anglers at the time, then put out a rule that no pike were to be returned. Thankfully they relented, digging a holding pool for the pike to be retained before being transferred to waters elsewhere. It was also about this time, I came across Mick Edwards landing a 25 pounder from the north bank, as I was walking by. Mick was getting excited thinking it was a thirty. It was the first really big pike from the water I'd seen. In mint condition showing possibilities of even bigger fish from the pit. I pleaded with Mick to put it back but he was fishing with another club member so he carried it round to the holding pool. The club finally came to its senses, telling us we could now return all pike over 10 pounds. In 1991 Bernard became a full Shell member and could fish the 'members only' island. In September '91 Bernard, fishing from the members island found an untapped hotspot and with hardly anyone fishing for the pike he went on to catch some magnificent bags of fish. Lots of big doubles, a fair few twenties topped by two different $28\frac{1}{2}$ pounders and a $30\frac{1}{2}$ pounder. He was able to fish for them exclusively on the island, the other members fishing there not twigging thinking he was catching carp. Then in May 1993 the cat was out of the bag, when the Shell angling club netted the lake. Bernard's $30\frac{1}{2}$ pound pike turning up in one of the sweeps bottoming out the 32 pound scales, the members present estimated the weight at 35 pounds showing the true potential of the Warren.

Up to then I was keeping a very low profile when piking the Warren; I did not use my backbiters for indicators as they are a sure sign of a pike angler. I would set the tackle up so it looked like I was carp fishing using a couple of Bitech Viper buzzers, and even fished with my old flags from years ago. The Shell angling club had started to net the Warren at the beginning of the close season to remove the large numbers of small carp that had gradually built up over the years, hoping it would give the remaining big fish a chance to pack on more weight. As the club members pulled in the net, Steve Davidson and Roger Harvey noticed a massive pike trapped in the mesh. The only scales available were an old set of Avons which the pike bottomed out easily. News of the fish soon spread amongst the regulars who fish the lake, one or two setting their sights on catching it. Steve Wells joined Bernard and I on the Warren at the start of the 1993-94 season in a joint effort to find out exactly what it did hold. Barry Summerhayes, a Shell member had also heard about the big pike netted through a friend of his, Dave Thompson. Barry said he was a bit sceptical at first but was soon convinced and had also set his heart on catching the monster. Barry had become a friend of Bernards, both being Shell members, and only living a few hundred yards apart. Bernard told me Barry was always trying to prise out of him where he was catching his big pike from, but at the time he wouldn't let on. Then when the club netted the lake Barry found he'd been sitting on the water all the time! As my mate, Steve Wells keeps telling me, "there are no friends in pike fishing, only associates". Sadly he's probably right on the modern big pike scene. With news of a big pike out the water soon got a hammering and the pike stocks suffered. So to save the quality of our fishing and more important the welfare of the pike it pays to play our cards close to our chest. With the big pike turning up in the net the Warren's secret was well and truly blown. What didn't help us also was the club treating the water for a weed problem (not a problem for me, I might add) - a small leaved lily with little yellow flowers that almost covered the lake. With most of the weed gone the roach, rudd and bream had nowhere to hide especially their fry which became an easy target for the pike. Rounding up large shoals the pike were driving them on to the surface along the margins. Hundreds of fry would leap clear of the water followed by a big swirl as the pike gave away their presence. Before, when the lilies covered nearly all the Warren a striking pike in the weed would have been mistaken for a carp. September 1993, and I was concentrating on an area called the 'Beach' fishing it a couple of times with Bernard and Steve for the morning before work and taking pike to over 20 pounds. October and we are fishing near the concrete block having much of the same with some good doubles. November and I was back on the 'Beach' and north bank where the pike were fry feeding in earnest. One morning Bernard, Steve and I were all playing doubles at the same time in the corner. My one being the smallest I dropped it back to photo Bernard and Steve with 18 and 16 pounders. With the pike fry feeding location was no problem, in fact the fishing was becoming easy. The only trouble was it encouraged more and more anglers to fish for the big predators. They had certainly packed on the weight with some good fish caught. Every time I had a run I was wondering if this was going to be the mid-thirty, thinking it was the ceiling for the lake. Then, in the middle of November it happened. I should have been on the Warren that day meeting Steve and Bernard, but something came up and I put Steve off, leaving Bernard to fish the water alone. Later in the morning Barry Summerhayes turned up having been thrown off his carp syndicate lake when it changed hands.

He would have been carping that day and wasn't too happy about losing his fishing. As one door shuts though fate was to be with him as another opens, and it certainly opened wide for him on that day. Barry had also been doing a bit of piking at the Warren, chasing the fry shoals round the lake. Bernard, fishing off the 'Beach' missed a run just as Barry arrived. Barry decided to ignore this area and headed for the long island type projection nicknamed "Southend Pier". There was room at the end for two anglers and as he walked along there was a young lad fishing and pike striking. Barry asked the lad how he was getting on. "No good, my baits keep falling apart". He reeled in and showed Barry one of his baits. He had a size 2 treble on what looked like 50lb wire, suspended below a massive bung. Impaled on the treble was a smelt with the guts hanging out. Barry took the lad under his wing giving him a couple of his traces and a dead roach, but by the time it had taken to re-set him up and cast out, the pike had moved over to the opposite bank. They were now swirling all along the north bank 50 yards away. It's a long walk round to the north bank, Barry decided but as the fry shoals had moved to the far side that's where he should be. By the time he got himself round there the fry had moved into the corner where the north bank meets the 'Beach', so this is where he set up. He didn't get a sniff of a fish, the fry and pike moving on. The pike had now begun to swirl in front of Bernard on the 'Beach', who was starting to pack away his gear. About three swims further on was Mick Edwards, who was carp fishing. He called Barry over telling him that a very large pike had swirled right under his rods and would he like to drop a bait in and try to catch it. Barry declined, moving another twenty five yards further along the bank to a large weedbed (where the big pike had been netted in the close season).

I'll let Barry tell what was to happen next. "I put one rod out with a small roach on a fry rig close to the surface and on the other rod I fished a sunken paternoster also with a freshly netted roach fry. Half an hour passed without so much as a swirl showing in the swim and I was beginning to think that we'd missed our chance. Mick had just made me a cup of tea and placed it in my hand when my drop back indicator bleeped once. I looked up and Mick's brother Gordon, the bailiff, was standing looking at the rods. It bleeped again as I walked over and he said that it had dropped back an inch or so. As I got to my rods I could see the one with the paternoster quivering. I wound down and set the hooks into what, at first, I thought was a jack, it just came straight in. The young lad I had met on the end of 'Southend Pier' and whose name was Stuart had sunk my 42" landing net in in anticipation. A huge head surfaced in front of him and everyone gasped. I thought it was a good upper twenty, Mick shouted it's a thirty! The pike decided that she was having none of it and went on a blistering run out into the open water for about 50 to 60 heart-stopping yards, what power! I was only using a 1¾lbs test rod and it was bent to it's limit, my 10lb Big Game line was singing in the breeze. The line was ripping from the baitrunner at an alarming rate but I decided that as she was running into open water I wasn't worried and wasn't going to rush this one. Several times she begrudgingly came to the net and off she went again, though each time the runs got shorter until she was boring to and fro along the bottom right in front of the waiting landing net. I told Stuart not to lift the net until her head touched the spreader block and even then he had to wiggle the net to get her huge tail in. As she went into the net Mick shouted "it's a forty!". All I knew was that I was exhausted, overjoyed, relieved, ecstatic, euphoric and bloody happy all at the same time. When I unhooked her my single size 10 treble was in her scissors. On my Avons she went 39lbs 8ozs, Mick was nearly right! At the time the club had a positive publicity campaign so I thought "sod it", as there were two bailiffs present there's no way I could keep it quiet. I rang the club secretary, Chris Emerson, who brought a set of Nash 50lbs scales and confirmed the weight of 39lbs 8ozs. I also rang my wife (who didn't realise how big 39lb was 'til she saw the pictures) my dad, who came from work, and my mate Dave Thompson who did the same. With the photo's taken I got into the water to release her. She swam off strongly towards the weedbeds. The icing on the cake was having my dad pull me out of the water and shaking my hand, congratulating me. I doubt that I'll catch a bigger one, but I'll keep trying for as long as I can keep fishing".

Well that's Barry's account of that historic day and the catching of his fabulous fish. Checking the photos when they were developed it was indeed the fish Bernard had caught two years earlier in September '91 at 30½lbs. She had put on another nine pounds in two years. Steve wasn't too happy when he heard of Barry's fish seeing I had put him off from fishing the Warren on that day. We reasoned now if she comes out again at the back end of the season carrying a bit of spawn she would be a good forty. With all the publicity of Barry's fish the Warren got a lot more attention from pike anglers, even some of the 'names' showing their faces on the water. At the back end of November, I was fishing the trout reservoirs having dates on Bewl Water, Bough Beech and Ardleigh. Looking at my diary I only managed three more morning sessions on the Warren in the run up to Christmas.

Then in December '93 the Warren threw up a 33 pounder, a pot bellied fish caught from the 'Southend Pier' area. There was also a 32 from the north bank, caught twice on two different days by the same angler. What with all the extra angling pressure the Warren was starting to give up some very good fish. At the time I wasn't too worried about neglecting the Warren as I was having some success on the trout reservoirs with fish to 34 pounds. Back on the Warren in February, John Smith had a cracking 32½ from the north bank and as the 1993-94 season came to an end a young lad caught a whopping 34 pounder from Gorse Island. The Warren had certainly blossomed with the capture of possibly three more different thirties, but the 39½lbs fish didn't show. With a lot more anglers targeting the big pike, casting baits all round the lake it was inconceivable that it had not been caught again. I believe if she was still alive she had hidden herself away for the winter laying up in one of the many bays or off one of the bars. Not moving far she could be picking off a 3 to 5 pound jack as it swam by, perhaps a big bream or tench even the odd duck now and again. At the start of the 1994-95 season I reckoned my best chance of catching the big pike is to fish the Warren from the start; the pike will be a lot more active so that's what I did. Topping up my selection of plugs from my local tackle shop, and in between snatching out the odd carp, I only cast out lures in June. Again I'm only fishing for a couple of hours before and after work. I start to search out all the cracks and crannies with the plugs taking a dozen pike to 12 pounds. Then, in July I fished a large dead natural sink and draw along the reed beds but apart from a fish weighing about 18 pounds that frightened the life out of me leaping clear of the water whilst trying to grab the bait as I lifted it out, the only other fish I caught that month were small.

By the middle of August enough was enough and I stopped playing at it and got down to some proper piking, ledgering a big chunk of air injected eel and a poly'd rudd. Fishing the logs area I dropped them either side of a bar I'd found. Both baits were taken within minutes, missing the run on the eel I caught a 15lbs on the rudd. Steve joined me next morning and we fished the same area where I had the 15. Again, I had a take on a poly'd rudd resulting in a 13 pounder, a stub nosed fished that was to come out to Steve and me three more times from different parts of the lake. Just before we had to leave for work Steve had a slow take and wound into a good fish. After a dogged battle I slipped the net under a nice looking 22 pounder. Things were looking good. Three days later I fancied fishing the 'Beach'. I'd been wanting to fish there from the start of the season but hadn't been able to get there for carp anglers. Pulling into the first car park I noticed there were still three bivvies on the Beach so I drove back round to the logs area. Again, dropping the baits on or just off the bar I had runs from the start, landing pike of 15, 14¾ and 8 pounds. I had started to photograph all the doubles I was catching now, trying to find out just how many doubles the Warren held. Checking the photos the 15 was the same 15 pounder I caught the first time I fished the bar. Returning next morning for a couple of hours again, I check out the 'Beach', the carp boys were still there. Disappointed I drove round to the second car park dropping in the corner giving the bar swim a rest. Within the first hour I had five runs missing three and landing two jacks; the corner was full of them, so for the last hour I moved back over to the bar. Dropping out a poly'd bream it was taken the second it hit bottom. Pulling into the pike straight away the fish moved off powerfully to my left, but applying side strain I was having trouble stopping it, moving fast just under the surface it was creating a big bow wave. Having to keep the rod up high so the line cleared the bull rushes I followed it round. Keeping the pressure on it finally started to tell and slowly I was playing her back. Is this the one I'd been looking for? Ten yards out I saw the pike for the first time, not the big one although still a big framed fish though badly marked up. Drawing her over the net I gently lowered her onto the unhooking mat. She was covered in small cuts and red marks. I could have cried, she had certainly been in the wars. Removing the single hook from the jaws I placed her into the weight sling, 27lbs 4ozs. Slipping her into a keepsack for a few minutes I was getting the camera out when Gordon the bailiff turned up. Gordon started to tell me about a pike caught a week ago in the corner, it had taken an anglers swim feeder as he wound in. The angler and his mate had somehow managed to land it and it was flapping about as Gordon walked by on the opposite side of the lake. Gordon said it was jumping about all over the gravel and he had shouted across to them to get it back into the water, he was told it weighed 32 pounds. "Well I don't know about 32 pounds", I tell Gordon, "I've got it in the keepsack and I make it 27lbs 4ozs". Gordon took a photo for me and we released her. As he carried on round the lake the eel section goes, a fish of $10\frac{1}{2}$ pounds. Steve was back fishing with me next morning, the 'Beach' was still occupied so we try the bay. Steve had four runs landing two jacks to 5 pounds. I missed a run off the island then took a $22\frac{1}{2}$ pounder on yet another poly'd bait, my second twenty from the Warren in two days. The next couple of visits turn out to be disappointing fishing. At the back of the lake we missed several runs, the culprits probably being jacks. When arriving at the Warren now the first thing I did was check out the 'Beach', but there were still no swims available. Steve and I found ourselves fishing the logs again casting baits out to the bar.

In the half light I had a 12 pounder on my eel. Eight o'clock and the poly'd bait was taken and I found myself playing a good fish. I managed to get it close a couple of times in the shallow water but Steve wouldn't get his feet wet to net it, but finally I have it close enough for Steve to net it from dry land. It turned out to be the marked up fish again, weighing just under 26 pounds, she had lost another pound and a quarter in a week. Releasing her now for a second time I pray and hope we don't see her for a while. At 42½ inches long to the fork of the tail she was one of the thirties that came out at the back end of last season. Two months into the new season with still no sign of the big fish I came off the Warren for a fortnight and returned in September. Bernard joined Steve and me now and my first fish back on the water turned out to be 'stub nose'. Steve had a small fish and Bernard caught two jacks from the back island. The next two sessions we concentrated in the corner and along the second car park bank, but apart from a mid-double that fell off when I tried to bully it into the net the only pike we did catch were jacks. The weather was starting to deteriorate, so with a bit of luck we might have a chance to fish the 'Beach' tomorrow.

Arriving in the half light the beach was deserted, the carp boys having vacated it at long last. Excitedly, I grab my tackle from the back of the car, scrambling down the slope I was dropping bits of it all over the bank. Do you think I could get a rod rest in, I must have tried at least 15 times in a couple of square yards, the gravel was like rock. Finally after about 10 minutes and a fair bit of cursing I managed to get four sticks in to a depth of two inches, leaning in all directions the carp boys would have shuddered at my set up. As I cast my first bait 50 yards out on to a shelf two cars pulled up behind me on the high bank, Steve and Bernard. I could hear Steve whinging along the bank having the same trouble as I did with the rod rests. Bernard's been on the 'Beach' before so he put his poles on a rod pod. Fishing with two rods each we had got the area well covered, I was extremely confident one of us was in with a chance of a good fish. 7 o'clock I had a pick up on the eel section but after a few seconds pulled out of what felt like a small pike. 8.30 and the poly'd rudd was taken by a fish of 5 pounds, Bernard and Steve have yet to register a run. The next two hours were spent drinking tea together and discussing the whereabouts of the big fish, is she still alive, and if so, where was she hiding? Then out of the blue at 10.30 my poly'd bait was taken again and line was slowly trickling off the spool. Striking into the fish I set the number 1/0 single and the rod goes over making a lovely curve

15lbs, it's the same 15 pounder I caught the first time I fished the bar.

On the beech at last and caught the pot-bellied fish at 25$^{1/4}$lbs.

and stayed there. My knees start to shake as the pike kited to the right taking line. It had been a long time since I'd had a knee trembler probably due to all the talk of the big fish a few minutes before. She was on the top now quite a way out just paddling about. I hate it when they come straight up on the surface as I'm always frightened they might shake the hook out. Slowly I steered her to Steve who was holding the waiting landing net, finally slipping her over the arms twenty yards further down the bank. Steve drew the net to the side and peered in. "It's a long fish Bill", he tells me as I joined him. Lifting her out of the landing net I lowered her onto the unhooking mat and removed the single hook from the scissors, she was indeed a long fish weighing 25¼ pounds. Running a tape from the tip of her nose to the fork of the tail showed 43½ inches. She was an unusual looking pike, big headed with a pot belly then dramatically tapering away towards the tail. She was unmistakably the pot bellied fish caught from 'Southend Pier' in December last year at 33 pounds. Checking the photos when they were developed later confirmed it. Over another 8 morning sessions in September, I gradually worked my way right round the lake. Catching three more doubles and a 20¼ from the second car park swim, making five twenties in four weeks. I'd had quite a lot of repeat captures now but there was still no sign of the big one. Carrying on behind the members-island I concentrated on an area where a large shoal of bait fish had congregated. Lots of small pike came to the rods with a few doubles, then in the middle of October, stub nose came out again to Steve. With all the repeat captures I was starting to have doubts, there cannot be too many pike we haven't caught, perhaps the big pike is dead? Calling it a day for the year I was beaten, but not defeated as I started my winter campaign on the big reservoirs giving the Warren a rest. With the ending of the formal close season, Shell angling club were going to keep the water open, so I decided to come back in May '95 and give it another shot for the elusive big pike. Winding up my fishing on the big reservoirs in March after 9 months of concentrated effort, I took 6 weeks out to recharge my batteries. It wasn't until the 3 May '95 that I had the urge to check out the Warren again. I found a lot of good carp moving round the back channel and not wanting to pike fish again just yet, I baited an area with a tin of luncheon meat then carried on walking round the lake. Returning an hour later creeping up to the swim I lowered a float fished piece of meat into the margin. The float cocked and ran across the surface. Striking the fish stopped it in it's tracks standing no chance with the heavy gear, pulling it to the side it was a tench about five pounds. The carp disappeared with all the commotion so dicing up another tin of meat I chucked it in, deciding to return early next morning. Arriving at the swim at dawn I quietly put in another tin of meat and lowered two floats close to some sunken branches. One hour later and I was on my way home well happy having taken carp of 17½, 14¾, 11¼ plus a 6 pound tench. I threw in two more tins of luncheon meat as I left, to keep the swim going until tomorrow. There were bushes to my left and a sunken tree to my right, fishing over the top of brambles I had about five square yards of clear water to play any hooked fish in. Making sure the landing net was in position and the rod rests set high enough so the line doesn't catch in the brambles, I gently laid my floats on the surface six inches from the sunken snags, with my hand hovering over the rods in anticipation. There were at least three carp digging in the swim giving themselves away with a stream of bubbles. One of the floats started to vibrate and slowly drift away from the other one as I lift the rod into the fish. Clamping down hard the carp still managed to make the first bush to my left. Sinking the rod well down in the water, I didn't try to bully it out holding it there to let it tire itself out for a minute or two. Submerging the landing net on it's side along the edge of the bush I pumped the carp towards it, the fish saw the net and dived in. Dropping the rod I grabbed the net arms with both hands swinging the carp out. Unfolding the mesh it was a twenty pound common, "Yes, yes", I shout doing an Irish jig round the fish. After all these years I'd finally caught my 20 pound common on a float two feet from the bank! Unbelievably I'd caught it in the exact spot where I had seen my first big common in the Warren all those years ago. Weighing 22½ pounds it was no monster by today's standards, but if it had weighed 40 pounds I couldn't have been any happier. Not doing a lot of carp fishing now I had promised myself a 20 pound common on a float and at long last I'd achieved it. Coming from the Warren it was even more pleasing, starting my fishing back on the lake with a high. Little did I know then that within weeks I would suffer one of my biggest lows ever, one that was to last six months. More and more carp moved round the back islands and channel now they had only one thing on their minds. Having caught my twenty, I let them get on with it and left them alone. My thoughts turned back to the pike in the lake, and the big one.

In the next two weeks while the carp were spawning in the reed beds, the few visits I made to the Warren I fished lures. Again, several small pike fall to my plugs up to a weight of 10 pounds. July, and the carp had finished spawning so I arranged to meet Bernard round the back of the lake for a morning's carping-come-piking. The 17th July 1995, the fateful morning arrived. Loading up the car with the tackle I remembered to throw in a pack of big deadbaits for the pike. Parking the car in the second car park I made my way round to a point near the concrete block. Fishing from this position you can cover any patrolling pike as they hunt the rudd shoals round the back island. There was also a good chance of a carp as they creep into a weedy bay that lays to the left of the point, when the sun's high in the sky. Dropping the gear in the swim I walked back the few yards to the corner of the weedy bay, throwing out handfuls of luncheon meat right in amongst the rushes hopefully setting a trap for the carp when they arrive later on in the day. Returning to my tackle on the point I put out a poly'd rudd to the left, close to a large weedbed. The other rod I lob another rudd the few yards to the reeds on the back island. Sitting back into the bed chair I looked round the lake for any sign of Bernard. The only other angler I can see is Mick Mills who was fishing off the end of members-only island, his white hat giving him away (the Bob Nudd of the carp world). The wind had started to pick up, funnelling through the point blowing across Gorse Island onto members island. Suddenly my right hand rod was away, striking into thin air I missed it completely not feeling anything at all. Quickly re-casting another bait to the same spot, I had just got the rod back on the rests when the line on the left hand rod was pouring from the spool. Winding down to the fish it feels like I'd pulled into a brick wall. I backwound for a couple of feet as the pike takes line then everything went solid. Leaning into the pike exerting tremendous pressure with the heavy tackle, something gives and I wind in a big ball of weed, the fish had gone. Clearing the weed from the line, I check the trace is okay and putting on another bait, dropped it five yards closer in away from the offending weedbed. Settling back in my chair I noticed Bernard making his way round on the opposite bank. "How's it going Bern", I shout across. "No good dad, I've checked out all the back channels and bays and haven't seen a single carp", he replied. "I reckon it's the strong wind keeping them down Bern, come on round and set up a pike rod there's plenty of room". "Had any runs Dad". "Yeah, two, I missed the first one then five minutes ago, I pulled out of a good fish when it weeded me". Bernard joined me on the point. "You say you had a good fish on Dad", Bernard asked as a big pike boiled right where I had lost the fish in the weed. "Did you see that

27¹ᐟ⁴ pounds covered in cuts and red marks. I could have cried.

22¹ᐟ²lbs, my second twenty from the Warren in two days.

John Smith with the Warren Monster weighing 32½lbs when he caught it in February 1994.

18 months later 50 pounds 12 oz. The markings are identical.

Dad", see it I'd half wound a bait in to cover it. Dropping it alongside the weedbed I put the rod in the rests only for the pike to come up again where I had removed my bait from, rewinding I cast it back to it's original position. "That didn't look a bad fish", Bernard said as he quickly started to change one of his carp rods over for pike. Seconds later the pike came up for a third time right in front of us, only this time it didn't go back down. The wind had become even stronger now making it difficult to make the pike out, showing a bit of back and dorsal fin, waving it's tail at me as it struggled to get beneath the surface. "Christ Bern that fish is in big trouble". "Yeah, it don't look too good Dad", Bernard replied as the pike drifted up against the reeds on the back island.

I could have easily cast a set of hooks across its back and dragged it in, but you don't do you. With the sun up now and more light penetrating the rippling water the pike looks long laying up against the rushes. "I reckon that's a good twenty Bern", (a good twenty, blimey if only I'd known). Mistake number one, number two was a little gem. "Dad, I'll have a walk round to the back island, I think I'll be able to reach the pike in the rushes and pick it out". "I wouldn't bother Bern, it will be blown on to members island time you walked round there", I tell him putting him off. It's another 15 minutes before the wind finally took it's toll on the weakening pike, moving it on towards members island. The last time I saw it the tail was still waving at me as it reached Gorse Island. Bernard had the time to pick it up at least three times before the wind shifted it, and to think I had stopped him. With the distressed pike surfacing in my swim it upset me somewhat making me lose my appetite for fishing on, so Bernard and I called it a morning and packed up. Walking back to the second car park we passed Gordon the bailiff doing his rounds. Bernard wanted to check out 'Southend Pier', so we drove round to the first car park for him to check it out. Ten minutes later I'm on my way home. Leaving the tackle in the kitchen I decided to go back to the Warren in the morning. Later jumping into bed I had a couple of hours sleep before having to go to work that night. Arriving home at 6.15 next morning, Sheila was up and waiting for me. I start to make up a flask. "You going over the Warren Bill?", Sheila asks me. "Yes my little petal only for an hour or so, can you make my flask up dear?". "Take the dog for a walk first Bill, I've got something to tell you". The dog's heard the word walk and has wrapped his legs round my foot. "Tell me what my love, I'll only be an hour the dog can wait", I say trying to shake him off my foot. "No you take him for a walk then I will tell you", Sheila said again more seriously. I'm wondering what's happened so thinking the worst I whizz Gizmo round the field in record time. "Well Min what the hell's happened?". "Mick Toomer phoned after you had left for work last night". "Oh, what did Mick want?", I ask Min feeling mighty relieved. "He's got a dead 50 pound pike in his bath". "He's got what?" "A 50 pounder in his bath", repeats Min.

"It's from the Warren ain't it Min?". "Yes how did you know?". I didn't answer. Standing there for several minutes I'm completely shell shocked. Finally coming back to my senses I picked up the phone and rang Mick forgetting its only just gone six. Mick answered half asleep. "Mick, it's Bill, what's all this about a 50 pound pike in your bath". "You've heard then, I picked it up last night, it had been found dying earlier in the day on members island. After it died it had been thrown onto the remains of an old fire, one side is completely wrecked covered in ash and gravel. When I picked it up I put it in the bath to wash it off". "What's the good side like Mick?". "I don't know it was late when I finally sorted it all out". "Go and have a look Mick". "Hang on for a minute Bill I'm still in bed, I'll go and check". "It looks good Bill in perfect condition, it's a monster Bill". "Right I'm on my way round Mick", "Give us ten minutes to get dressed mate". Ringing Steve Wells who was also on nights, I tell him the story and would he like to join me to see the monster. On the way round to Micks I fill Steve in about me and Bernard's morning on the Warren, and our encounter with the big fish.

Mick greeted us and took us to the bathroom. As I go through the door my eyes nearly popped out as I caught sight of it. My breath taken away, laying there she's completely filling Mick's Jacuzzi. A colossus of a pike it was huge, a true monster absolutely mind blowing. I felt like getting in the bath with her as I gently run my hand down the pike's side. Steve and I help Mick to carry her down to the garden for some photos before she takes her final journey to the taxidermist. I remembered to slip a tape measure in my pocket as I left home, being important to have some accurate measurements of this historic fish. Steve held the tape on her nose as I ran it to the tip of the tail, length 51 inches. To the fork of the tail $48\frac{1}{2}$ inches, girth 29 inches. Trying to hold her up for a good photo was almost impossible as my hands sunk into her massive girth. Christ knows how you would have coped if she was alive. Her flabby stomach was completely empty, this is no exaggeration you could have easily stuffed a ten pound pike inside and you wouldn't have known it was there. Mick later accurately weighed her on a brand new set of

Reuben Heaton 60lb scales and registered 50lb 12oz. Returning home, three times I climbed into my bed trying to sleep only to get up again as the events of the last two days come flooding back into my mind. Why did she die, obviously an old fish with only two big main teeth left, but she looked like a new pin. Where had she been hiding all this time? Was it the good fish I pulled out of in the weed, where five minutes later she first surfaced? Oh, why did I stop Bernard from going round to pick it out? I'm wondering how many anglers would have fished it out, then claimed the record. For the next couple of days I was walking round like a zombie, not able to work, sleep or eat. Returning to work my mates couldn't believe I'd taken time out over a fish. I tried to explain to them the importance of the pike and how I'd spent all my life fishing for such a fish. How it was Britain's first authenticated 50 pound pike in modern times. Imagine a stamp collector, I told them, sorting through a pack of cheap stamps he'd bought and finding a Penny Black. He's got as much chance as a gardener has of collecting a bag of rocking horse manure. We are talking 50 pound pike and I was that close. To this day I can still close my eyes and see that big tail waving to me, as she slowly drifted away to that big pond in the sky.

She's completely filling Mick's jacuzzi!

Talking to Mick Mills sometime later he said it was he who had netted the pike out on the members island. "At first I thought it was a big carp tangled in weed I could just see some back, it kicked free of the weed and went down only to come up again on it's side. It went down for a second time but again it surfaced. This time it rolled over and died. It was sometime later I netted it out and asked Army John if he had any scales as mine only weighed up to 33 pounds. John hooked the pike under the chin and lifted recording a weight of 48 pounds". Talking to Mick Toomer about the weight difference he said as far as he knows the pike was weighed on five different set of scales during the day with five different weight readings from 47 to 55lbs. There was also talk the pike may have taken in water Well I don't know anything about that, what I do know is it had nothing in it when Steve and I photographed it round Micks. As for absorbing it through the skin, how much is anyone's guess in those short hours. I also learned I had missed out again the morning the pike died. Gordon Edwards told me when he first come across the fish he had shouted his lungs out round the lake for me, but unfortunately I had just left. Although I was devastated when I first saw her dead in Mick's bath, the one good thing to come from this sorry tale, I had felt very privileged to have cradled such a magnificent pike in my arms.

A Twist to the Tale

A week later when the angling weeklies came out with the photos of the big pike plastered all over the front covers, I received a phone call that left me speechless. It was Barry Summerhayes. "Bill listen, I don't think that's my fish". "Don't be silly Barry of course it's your fish", I tell him. "Bill I've checked my photos and I'm telling you it's a different fish, I believe it's the one you caught off the 'Beach' last year". "Don't be daft mate, it wouldn't have packed on all that weight in a year". "Well whatever one it is, it's definitely not my one", Barry insisted. "I'll check my photos", I tell Barry putting down the phone. I'd not bothered to check before because like everyone else I assumed the dead pike was the 39½ that Barry and earlier Bernard had caught. Quickly going through my photos I checked out Bernard first holding the 30½ when he caught it in '91, but unfortunately they all showed the wrong side, the side of the big dead pike that was badly damaged. Checking some cuttings of Barry's 39½ again they didn't show the side I was looking for, although again I matched Barry's fish with Bernards. Next I checked out the pot bellied pike I caught from the 'Beach', and I must admit at first glance it looked the same. I could see now how it had Barry

188

over, the markings almost identical. Later even Wayne Sutton was convinced it was the same fish until I got the magnifying glass out but again it wasn't the fish.

Back on the phone to Barry I asked him if he had photos of the 39½ showing both sides. "Bill it's the fish John Smith caught off the north bank", he answered. "You sure Mate?", I replied trying to think back to when John had caught his pike. Barry went on, "I also phoned John Smith telling him the dead pike wasn't the one I had caught. He wouldn't believe me at first Bill, telling me like you did earlier that it just had to be. Then he checked his photos of the 32½ he had caught with the photos in the Angling Times and they were identical to the dead one". Several seconds passed before I finally answered. "Blimey Barry do you realise there still could be another monster swimming about in the Warren mate, if your 39½ isn't dead". My brain goes into overdrive as I try to take it all in. If Barry's fish is still alive and weighed 39½ when John caught his weighing 32½, then 18 months later John's pike turns up found dying at 50 pounds what weight could the 39½ be now? I know the weight of a big fish can go down as well as up, but the possibilities were absolutely mind blowing.

Bernard obtained a print of John Smith's pike from Barry, it matched perfectly with my photos of the dead monster. So for the last 18 months I and a lot of other anglers had been fishing for not one big fish but two. Later I asked John to tell me the story of the day when he caught it from the north bank. John told me it was a work mate, John Russell who first put him on to the pike in the Warren, then showed him the way to do it by catching a 29½. John went on, "It was three months later, 12 February 1994, I was to have my day. Fishing off the north bank there was a cold wind blowing into my face. 2.30 in the afternoon my big dead rudd paternostered close in was taken. Striking into a big fish it came straight up on to the surface and into the net in one minute flat. On the scales she weighed 32½ pounds. John's fish didn't come out again until she was found dying on members island. How it managed to pack on all that colossal amount of growth and weight in 18 short months without being captured again tells me, probably, like the 39½ she must have been feeding on very large prey. Seeing there's still a possibility of Barry's pike being alive we decided to keep the information we'd found out to ourselves. Giving us a slight chance of perhaps a truly remarkable pike. Also by not letting Joe Public know, so soon after the death of the 50 pounder, it would save the Warren from being flogged to death. As

Mick, Steve and me with the fish that I could only have dreamed about.

Awesome.

you can imagine for the next three months I spent a fair bit of time fishing the Warren catching another thirty pike to 18½ pounds. Barry and Bernard's pike has still not been seen dead or alive since Barry caught it in November '93. Also I find my enthusiasm for fishing is starting to wane for some unknown reason.

October '95, and I began my winter campaign on Ardleigh. Fishing with Steve I was lucky to have a 22½ on my first trip. But even Ardleigh seems to have lost its magic for me, I'm finding it harder to make the effort to go out. Making up excuses, it's too windy, cold, too much colour, you name it, I said it. Looking back I think the circumstances leading up to the death of the big Warren pike had a bigger effect on me that day than I first thought, draining away all the enthusiasm and pleasure I normally get from my fishing. Christmas comes and goes, the weather is diabolical with strong easterly winds that have been with us for months. The reservoirs freeze over, thaw out then freeze over again. In the last two months with the weather being so bad my enthusiasm was at a low ebb. I'd only fished two half days. Then at long last after about six months I finally managed to get the big pike out of my system, putting it in perspective. With the monster turning up in the Warren it's probably the best thing that has happened on the pike scene for a long time. I find after all my years piking and time spent on the Warren I didn't know it all, thank God. If a small gravel pit in Essex can produce a 50 pound monster and could still have another one swimming about in there, then there's a chance for all of us. Who knows it might be your pit, lake or reservoir that turns up the next monster. Every time you have a run, feel that line pulling through your fingers it could be another big one, the unknown. The magic is back, and the boat tackle is back out and cleaned, I can't wait to get to Ardleigh before it closes for the season. The rain is coming down in stair rods as I push away from the bank at first light, six hours later I haven't had a run and it's still pouring down. Midday and I'm starting to have second thoughts, perhaps I was a little hasty with the returning enthusiasm, me thinks, as the rain runs down the back of my neck. It wouldn't have taken much for me to call it a day, hang on one of the floats is gone. "Damn, missed it". Blimey that's a good fish just boiled to my left, I swing the boat round to cover it with the baits. Five minutes later I return a 20½ followed by a nice looking 27½, then as the light started to fade after catching a couple of smaller fish I finished with a 23.

This old wrinkly is well and truly back and firing on all cylinders. It's the

The Warren Monster with Kim, the taxidermist.

27¹ᐟ²lbs, the best of three twenties; it's the fourth occasion I've been lucky to have caught three in a day.

36¹ᐟ²lbs and a new personal best for me from Ardleigh.

What could have been....

fourth occasion I've been lucky enough to have caught 3 twenties in a day, so there are still one or two fish left in this old piker yet. Mind you my very next trip to the Warren was a disaster. It's absolutely freezing as I pulled up in a deserted car park, finding I'm the only one daft enough to be out on such a cold day. I'm supposed to meet Bernard and Steve to see if the pike have moved on to the shallows. Walking round the lake the bitter easterly wind is cutting right through me. Ice is forming in the margins as I walked out into the water to put the rod rests in. Freezing water nearly reaches my knees before the shock hits me. In my eagerness to get to the swim this old fool forgot to put his moon boots on! Wringing out my socks I'm drying my numbed feet as Bernard arrives. Ten minutes later Steve turned up with his dog, giving the fishing a miss he's just come out for a walk in the grim conditions. All the feeling has left my feet, I believe frost bite had set in. Taking some deadbaits out of my tackle bag I'm going to impress Steve by putting on a whole jumbo mackerel. Opening the Tescos carrier bag I pulled out two pairs of kippers, I've taken them out of the freezer by mistake. I'm starting to lose it again!

Well that's about it with one hundred and one stories untold, but I would like to finish this section with two photos of Warren fish. Both taken on the same roll of film which brings the book nicely full circle. One shows a wrinkly old piker with one welly in the grave holding the magnificent Warren monster - the past. The other a young angler, my grandson Darrell with a small jack which could easily be one of the big pike's offspring - the future.

Perhaps the culmination of my pike fishing days.

But just the beginning of his!

10

......AND BEYOND

In August 2004 I received a letter from Ric Franklin asking if I might consider doing a reprint of the book. Ric used to be the R.O for the P.A.C in Suffolk and a few years ago I had done a talk and slide show for his region. He had wanted some more books for the members, and one for himself. Ric used to lend out his to the young anglers to encourage them and inevitably had lost a few, including Dimples to Wrinkles. Unfortunately all my copies had been sold. Anyway Ric had found himself in the position of needing a new career, and decided to have a go at publishing. The main bit of his business aiming at academic and special interest books, but as a labour of love he was interested in getting an angling imprint going. As a project, he indicated he would be happy to take on costs, paying me royalties on sales etc and would welcome my thoughts. Talking to a few of my mates about my book I asked them on their thoughts about me doing a reprint; add an extra chapter they all told me. An extra chapter, blimey I didn't think I would still be fishing let alone doing a reprint with an extra chapter seven years on. Right the lads have given me the thumbs up so lets go for it then, chapter 10.

It's the 28-9-1996 I am sitting on the banks of Ardleigh reservoir in Essex. I have just landed a new personal best pike, and I am in a daze. Cradled in my arms is 4 feet and half an inch of fighting pike weighing 36lbs 8 oz. After 50 years of fishing where do I go now? Where do I go... forward, I want a lot more of this!

The next twelve months turn out to be a bit of an anti climax with just one more twenty from Ardleigh and one from Abberton. My best fish possibly being a 3lb 6oz crucian carp from the Warren what a bait (only joking). Then in November 1997 I have a day up on Darwell Reservoir in

Sussex run by the Hasting Fly Fishers, the reservoir had thrown up one or two big pike in the past. On a couple of previous visits Steve wells, Tony Corless, Doc James Gardner, Andy Walker and I had caught the odd twenty with some good size doubles. On one of those days Steve had taken Fred his Dad with him, Fred going on to catch a massive pike weighing 33lb 8oz. I think Steve was quite pleased, mind you he hasn't taken his Dad out since, pike fishing that is. Didn't Steve mention earlier in the book that there are no friends in pike fishing, only associates, well it seems in Steve's case it's family too.

Steve Wells helping dad, Fred hold his 33lb 8oz Darwell Reservoir pike.

Anyway going back to the day in question, I had teamed up with Tony Corless and we were trolling the margins with an electric motor (3.H.P minn kota) , using float fished live trout. We found the margins were full of tree stumps, most reservoirs are valleys dammed at one end and the stumps have been left after the trees were felled before the reservoirs are flooded. The stumps making an ideal ambush point for pike to hit the trout as they swim by. The only problem with fishing the margins, being that every now and again one of our rigs may catch a snag or stump. When a float disappeared what we would do is feel down to see if it was a fish, if not we would reverse the boat back over the snag and pull down from the opposite direction hopefully freeing the rig. Using braid or strong nylon 99.9% of rigs are recovered suffering just the odd broken or bent treble.

Tony and I were using two rods each and the floats were well spread. On one of my reels the spool was loaded with 30 pound bait braid on the other 15 pound big game line. After landing a small fish and missing a run, my float with the big game on slowly sunk down. I start to reel and feel at the same time to see if it's a fish, it felt snagged. Tony starts to reverse the boat, as I curse winding up the other rods. As we work back over the snag to pull my rig free from the opposite direction, some slack line on my snagged rod gets caught around the engine prop and dragged inside the casing. Seeing the line is damaged I decide to bite through the big game line and set about trying to retrieve the baited rig by hand. Wrapping fives turns of line around my hand I start to pull, suddenly something is pulling back twice as hard nearly wrenching my arm from its socket.

"It's a bloody big fish Tony." I scream as my hand then my arm is pulled into the water. The line is now starting to cut deep into my hand as the pike tows me, Tony and the boat around the reservoir. Good job it's the rod with the big game line on, if it was the rod with braid I might have lost some fingers. Eventually with a lot more cursing and screaming from me and a lot of help from Tony we located the loose end of line and tied three shoddy knots to the line back on the rod. Freeing my now blue hand, I wind down quickly to get the tangle and knots on the reel. The rod then slammed over and the knots were pulled back into the water, as I have to give line. I thought that was it but once I got them back on the rod I started getting the upper **hand!**

As the pike surfaced alongside the boat Tony netted her first time, who was a lucky boy then. The weight of the pike 28lb 12oz, my biggest hand pike caught to date (I wouldn't recommend it though).

It was around this time Oct-Nov 1997 that Neville Fickling asked if I would be interested in contributing to a list of successful pike anglers in the UK. Having already had the agreement in principle of Dave Horton, Eddie Turner, Mick Brown, Jim Housden and Nige Williams.

What a nest of hornets dear Nev has stirred up with this one over the years. I must admit to enjoying keeping records of my pike, and looking back on what I've caught. Keeping accurate records will help you catch pike in the future. Nev decided to call it *The notable pike anglers big fish list* and he's still updating it to the present day. Personally I would like to see what other pikers are catching. Mind you, there's a lot of anglers out there with impressive lists of pike who like to keep their catches to themselves, not wanting the publicity. There are others who say anglers will keep on catching the same old pike just to add to their tally on the list, and the pike will suffer. Come on lads its only a list; it will never be a true record but it will show future generations of pikers what some of us caught in years gone by. I did ask Nev if my hand caught pike counts and he said yes as I played it out on my rod, that's very generous of him (did I say generous!).

In the 1999-2000 season I found myself spending more and more time on

The Darwell hand played 28lbs 12oz.

Norfolk and Suffolk rivers, The Waveney, Yare and others. Fishing with Steve Wells using a boat we have had some brilliant days piking, mainly trolling lives. What we would do first was motor down river using a fish-finder looking for a shoal of bait. Then we would drop the anchor at one end of the boat in mid river up stream of the shoal. Letting out rope with the boat side on to the flow we then drove to the bank tying up the other end of the boat to a tree or the rushes. I would then use a big bait-dropper tied to a spool of line to drop 3-4 lots of maggots and hemp down into the swim, topping up every 10 minutes. Using our roach rods we would then start trotting our floats down the current to the shoal of bait, also a couple of our pike rods would be put out. Some days the bait fishing would be so good that at times the pike fishing became a secondary concern. There was even one day when the bait was bigger than the pike. It was while bait fishing at the river Waveney, Steve hooks into something big on his roach rod, he was using two maggots on a 16 hook to 3lb line. For 15 minutes the fish plods under the boat, Steve not able to get it off the bottom. Another 10 minutes pass and Steve thinking its probably a pike said, "I will give it the big one, if it comes off its comes off."

I told him to take it easy, after all this time I would like to see it. Ten minutes later I slip the net under a 21lb mirror carp, how it never swam out into the fast current or into the rushes pulling free I will never know. Bait

Steve Wells with a 21lb bait.

21lb, best pike on the day 18lb 8oz.

With a bucket full of bait we would then start trolling for the rest of the

day. On some of the days we would have up to 20-30 runs with as many as a dozen doubles in the boat, hopefully with a twenty or two now and again. It doesn't get much better than that.

Looking back mind you, over the years if we had plotted up all of the time just fishing dead baits, I am sure we would have caught a lot more, bigger fish. But hey, it wouldn't have been half as much fun. Talking of catching bigger pike, on the rivers we found that using bigger than average size baits sorted out some of the better pike for us, the bigger the bait the better. I know I might upset one or two anglers here but it's a fact big pike eat big bait. In the last couple of years, if Steve and I catch a jack of a pound or two it will go on one of our rods. A large roach, perch or a big bream too. We found trolling a big bait is no problem the baits fish well and just a bit bigger than average pike float is needed. As long as the bait is fished away from the bottom no trouble. You wont get many takes mind you, being selective on the pike you are fishing for, but if you do get a run there will be no mistaking it; it will be quite spectacular, and I mean spectacular. The pike will hit it

Steve Wells with a Jack caught upper twenty. The boat in the background is Dave Horton's, just before he catches our anchor rope, and throws all his pike floats out of the boat.

hard and fast, the reel screams as the line is a blur as its ripped off the spool. How do we rig up and strike using the bigger baits you might ask. We fish a 3 hook set up with a large single or a size 4 treble in the nose of the bait, about 4-6 inches back a no. 4 treble just laying alongside the bait, and the last treble nicked in by the vent. As soon as the pike takes, all the other rods are quickly wound up, the boat is then steered right over the sunken float, no waiting. With your boat partner hovering over the side of the boat with the net at the ready, you wind down hard pumping the rod all at the same time. Hopefully your partner will scoop the pike up with the net, as the fish hits the surface. Nine times out of ten it will open its mouth flaring the gills while she shakes her head. Throwing the hooks and bait in the net, as the water is boiled to foam.

I have seen Steve go as white as a sheet and be completely drained after one or two encounters with old Esox. The fight might only last a few seconds, but the anticipation before you wind down is mind blowing. Probably the most exciting few seconds a piker will experience.

Steve has fallen in love with the rivers of Norfolk so much so that he has brought a holiday home on the banks of the river Yare at Brundall, also a small hardy cruiser.

Do yourself a favour and book his bungalow up for a week's piking, you will not be disappointed.

Turning back to my diary the 2000-2001 season was a strange one, with 232 pike caught, 71 of them being doubles with only one twenty. Fishing mainly waters that had produced a good stamp of pike to me over the years, the ratio worked out for every 10 doubles caught one would be a twenty. For the amount of doubles for this season I would have expected to have caught about seven twenties. Mind you looking back at my records I did have a few big doubles in the 18-19 pound range, also I seemed to have pulled out of one or two good pike that year for no particular reason. Perhaps it was just one of them seasons we all have now and again.

To prove my point checking my records for the 2001-2002 season, fishing on the same waters in the main my record was, 197 pike caught (35 less), 90 doubles, (19 more), 12 twenties (a big 11 more). So as you can see although I had caught less pike, the average size was a lot bigger resulting in the 11 additional twenties. A couple of days on Chew Valley probably helped with a few better pike, Steve and I getting on the trout reservoir on day four.

The water had a reputation for throwing up some tremendous bags of pike for the lucky anglers who managed to get on the reservoir on the first couple of days. News coming back down the grape vine, was of boats having five and seven twenties with lots of back up fish and also a number of thirties being caught. Steve and I were biting at the bit; 400 miles round trip for a days pike fishing and we couldn't wait to get there. Unloading the tackle in the car park we met Dave Kelbrick and his mate, who had fished the water on one of the first days. Catching five twenties I believe and also having lots of other big pike follow their lures to the boat. Not only that, they had caught a shed full of back up fish into double figures. Dave was good enough to fill us in on what had been caught, pointing us in the right direction, there was also talk of a 38lb out.

It was late when we finally got underway, what with all the bags being

A river 27lbs 12oz on a big bait.

thoroughly searched by the reservoir staff from Bristol water, looking for lives and and illegal baits, the reservoir only allowing sea dead baits and lures.

Leaving the jetty at wood ford lodge we open up the outboard motor and head down the reservoir making for stratford bay, about 10 other boats out of the 30 or so there do the same. On reaching the bay we drop the anchor in 10 feet of water, about 50 yards from the bank. We found the reservoir is full of fry up to 3-4 inches long, no wonder the killing lure is a small silver spoon. Steve wastes no time in casting a spoon 30 yards toward the bank, half way back the rod's bent over and he is playing a good double first cast. Clipping on a small silver and copper spoon, I start to search the main body of the reservoir. On my third cast I join Steve with a nice fish weighing about 18 pounds. Looking around at the other boats fishing the area, the pike are coming thick and fast. A few minutes later I am into my second pike of the day, "could be a twenty" I tell Steve as she goes into the net, 20lbs 8oz. After a quick photo Steve's playing another big double, it's unbelievable fishing. Gradually the takes slow down as all the feeding fish in the area are probably caught, and we have to start to work harder for the pike.

25lbs and from Chew, caught on a 2.5 inch spoon.

Late in the afternoon, after four more doubles are landed to our boat, my rod goes over and stays there.

"This could be a good fish steve" I say, there is no kicking of the rod just a heavy weight. The pike surfaces and starts to circle the boat, I start to panic as I see the width across the pikes back. I can see the spoon quite clearly hanging outside the jaws, the hooks just nicked in the scissors, as she paddles just out of reach of the waiting net. Ever so gently I pull her towards us and as she goes over the arms Steve swings her safely into the boat. Laying the pike in the weigh sling, the scales are pulled down to just over 25 pounds. Not as big as I had first thought, the width of the back having me over, but still a very nice fish. As we were heading back to the jetty by wood ford lodge at the end of a marvellous days fishing, I tot up the pike I have caught, 12 pike, 10 doubles and two twenties.

My second day on the reservoir can't come quickly enough, but unfortunately I was to miss out. It was for the following year's fishing on Chew, Steve and I had again managed to get there for the first few days. Being very fortunate to have drawn 2-3 of October, then again on the 16-17 of the same month. I was fishing the Warren at the time and had just pulled out of a good fish right at the net. The start of a bad day, as I rebaited Sheila phoned, telling me the hospital had been trying to get in touch with me. Apparently there had been a cancellation and if I wanted to take it up I had to be in hospital for 11 o clock next day, to have my nose operated on. (more on the nose later).

"I cant make it Sheila I am going to Chew for the next two days with Steve", I tell her.

"Well you better phone the hospital and tell them", she replied.

For the next two hours I sit there weighing up what to do, hospital or Chew, nose or pike. After a lot of soul searching I finally decide on hospital, I have still got two more days on Chew later in the month I tell myself. It might be as long as a year before I get another opportunity to have my operation, Christ only knows how big my nose would have got by then. Telling Steve of my decision, he phones Jason Davis to see if he will accompany him to Bristol waters in the morning.

Two weeks later with a bloody big plaster across my nose, I am heading back to Chew with Steve. First day on the water is very hard work for very little, the reservoir having had a lot of pressure over the last two weeks. Although I did have a good perch of 3 pounds at the jetty, I finished the day with three small pike and one double.

Second day on the reservoir we start off again in Stratford bay trolling smelts, working our way to Herriots then back to Stratford bay. As we troll around for our third pass one of my floats disappears, I am into a good fish on one of the smelts. After a spirited fight we are weighing a 22lbs 8 oz pike,

Just out of hospital with a Chew twenty, and a plastered nose.

success right away. Trolling back over the same area we have another two doubles on the smelts, we found the pike were laying up in a large weed bed. By trolling our floats right along the edge of the weed we are picking off the odd pike. When the runs finally dried up we started to work our way around the reservoir and as we slowly trolled along I started to cast out a spring dawg on the lure rod. Suddenly the rod loops over and down into the water and I find myself playing another good double. Steve decided he would like a bit of the action so we started taking it in turns on the lure rod, Steve getting stuck in with a 19lb. Later in the day I was to be lucky again, catching another twenty on the spring dawg. What a brilliant days fishing on the reservoir, with another brace of twenties and 6 doubles. Unfortunately there was talk that the reservoir was going to open up for fly fishing in the summer for the pike , not such a good idea. So I decided I would probably give Chew Valley a miss next season. As it happened it wasn't a good decision on my part, as you will see later in the chapter.

In between our visits to Chew, Steve and I had been doing a bit on the Fen drains and also the Cut Off channel. Mind you for us, some of the drains are a pig of a journey, there is a certain one that I have not come home from there the same way twice.

Steve with the 26¹/²lb pug nose pike, no nose comments please!

But for all the aggro of the travelling, the fishing at times was well worth the effort. Steve wells catching on one of his sorties a stunning fish, a pug nose pike weighing 26lbs 8oz.

We even had a couple of days on the notorious black dyke intake on the Cut-Off channel. On one of the days sharing a catch of 25 doubles with Steve, my share being 15 doubles averaging 15lbs up to a weight of 21lbs 8 oz. Looking back Steve and I were unlucky to have missed out on a couple of big pike when we fished the Fens at that time.

The first was on the drain that we always got lost on our way home from. One of my mates Roy Lyons had caught the same 30 pound pike up to a weight of 32lbs 8 oz, three times over two seasons from the water. Steve had been unlucky having netted it twice for Roy, then again for Steve Biggs a year later when she had gone down in weight to 28lbs 8oz. The second time we missed out big time, and I mean big time, it was on a drain we had fished on and off for a number of years. The last time we had been on the drain was when we had a days fishing with Steve Biggs and Rob Christen. We all went on to have a very nice day with plenty of pike to 18lbs.

Roy Lyons with the drain pike he caught 3 times to $32^{1/2}$lbs, over two seasons.

Steve Biggs with the big 'un at 38lbs 6oz.

The following year whilst pike fishing the boat yards at Brundell on the river Yare, we received a phone call from Steve Biggs.

"Bill I have just had a call from Rob he has just caught a 39lbs plus pike from the drain, wants me to go down and do the photos."

Me and Steve were speechless. What a turn up, it's almost unbelievable it must be the pike of the season. Rob Christens fish becoming a new fenland pike record. Rob went on to catch her again at around 37lbs. After Rob had caught her we could have so easily gone onto the drain and fished for her ourselves, but with all the publicity and pressure on the pike we gave it a swerve.

Mind you I was truly pleased for Steve Biggs though, when he caught her at 38lbs plus having been on the water with Rob for a number of years.

Then in the January Nige Williams turns up on the drain and catches her again at a weight of 38lb 4oz. Only Nige I believe could gather all the information from the grape vine, put it all together, then come down and catch her first trip.

It's the 16th of September 2004, I have decided to have a few days fishing on Abberton, and while there try to add 2-3 more pages to the additional chapter of this book. But what with the good company and all the pike activity I have had little chance. Sitting on the culvert wall on the reservoir, I am struggling to put two words together. The last two paragraphs have taken me about six hours.

First I had a double on a rudd fished on a paternoster in the culvert, then I missed a run on a drifter, followed by a small fish again to a rudd fished on a paternoster. The reservoir is full of weed, and I am fishing the rod with the drift float set at 6 feet in 12 feet of water. Using dead roach for bait (I have no lives) it's proving to be a quite successful method, having just caught two more doubles on it. There is a big bank of floating weed to the right of me, about 30 yards out, I was sure there was one or two pike laying underneath. After awhile the wind picked up and starts to move it. Grabbing my lure rod I cast a spring dawg right up to the edge of the moving weed. The rod goes over and I'm playing my fourth double to the bank. An hour later I have yet another double on the drifter.

At one o clock Chris Cade turned up to fish the afternoon, Chris asked me if I would be renewing my ticket for Abberton?

"I doubt it Chris, what with only fishing the reservoir about six times a year, and then only for a few hours," I tell him. "At 100 pounds it's not really worth it, I can always get a guest ticket in the future mate."

"Well I can always get one for you," Chris replied. "Anyway Bill, how has it been fishing this morning?"

"It's fishing really well mate," I say as I show Chris half the scribble on the fen drains I have managed to write down, telling him I have been trying all morning to put together a page or two for the book.

"I think I better get off home and try to do some more work on it," I tell him.

As I pack the gear into the car I leave the rods fishing to the last, slowly winding them in, the paternoster first.

Picking up my last rod the one with the drifter on, I look across the reservoir. Bloody hell the floats gone. Winding down until I could wind no more, I pull into the fish. The rod goes over and stays there, it feels a half decent pike I think to myself. A couple of minutes later the fish is close to the bank, as Chris comes down to the bank to have a look.

"You going to hand it out for me Chris?" I ask.

"I don't think so, look at the size of the head, I think I will go an get the net," Chris replied.

Was this last minute Abberton pike trying to tell me something?

"You're right mate, it could be a twenty it looks close to me," I say.

With the pike on the unhooking mat I asked Chris if he didn't mind taking a photo, seeing as it might possibly be my last pike from Abberton reservoir.

As I am driving the 30 miles home, a journey that takes about 45 minutes, my mind is starting to go back in time, on all the good years of piking I have been lucky to have spent on the big reservoir called Abberton. With the good days on the water coming and going in my head, I start to have second thoughts about giving up my ticket. Was that last minute pike on the drifter trying to tell me something. Sod it, after all the good years I have spent on the reservoir, I just might give it another season.

Sorry for the distraction, but I believe Abberton could still prove very important for me in the future. Wasn't I struggling to put some words together for the book at the time. The reservoir then coming good, giving me enough material for another half a page. Even as I left the water, didn't one of the lads shout "It's good to see are still alive and kicking bill." It gave me a shot in the arm, mind you I don't kick so high now, my knees and ankles are starting to go.

Going back to my fishing registers, it was at the back end of 2002 that I had a fantastic six days out of 12 one of my local gravel pits. I had been ground baiting the pit heavily every 3 days for two months, putting in chopped up mackerel and big chunks of naturals. It all came good on my birthday, fishing from first light with Roy Lyons. We hadn't had a run between us in the first four hours, then at mid-day my mackerel tail goes. A short while later I am cuddling my birthday pike weighing 24lbs 12oz, its Friday the 13-12-2002, unlucky for some but not for me.

Three days later I am back, and two baits are quickly cast out into the swim, one with mackerel tail the other eel. At 9 o'clock the mackerel tail rod's away, pulling into the fish it feels heavy, just holding deep down in front of me. Exerting more pressure she surfaces, and I slip her into the waiting net. Unhooked and in the weigh sling she looks enormous, the dial goes round 33 lbs 8oz, yes, yes! Photos done I give her one more admiring look, as I gently release her back to her home. Before leaving I chop up another 2-3 pounds mackerel, and catapult it out into my going swim.

Next day I returned to the pit with Roy, after 8 hours fishing without a run I decided to call it a day and go home. Roy said he would fish on for a little bit longer. On reaching home Sheila told me Roy had just phoned to

Who's a happy boy then? 33lb 8ozs!

say he had caught a 34lbs 8oz pike in the dark. It turned out to be the 33lbs 8oz fish I had the day before. It must have gone straight back out to the baited area I had topped up, and put on another pound in weight, giving Roy a new personal best. I should be so lucky, my repeat captures normally lose a bit of weight.

It was another four days before I am back on the pit with Roy. In the meanwhile I had a day on Abberton on the 19-12-2002. It was not a bad day on the reservoir, catching seven pike, including three doubles up to 14 pounds.

Getting back to the pit, two rods are cast out into the baited area, again fishing one with mackerel, the other with eel. With no runs in the first couple of hours to me or Roy, I decide to do something different. Making up a third rod I drop a float fished eel section close in. At mid-day the float lifts then lays flat on the surface; I strike straightaway not wanting to deep hook the pike, resulting in a nice fish of 18lbs. I hook up another bit of eel (head section) and drop it back in the same spot. Twenty minutes later the float's running into the rushes, it turns out to be a fish weighing 23 pounds. Just before I leave for home I topped up the swim with more bait, Roy had missed out but came good with a twenty next day.

Two days later it was raining quite hard. It had turned 2 o'clock before Roy turned up, mind you he hadn't missed anything. Checking my watch, it had just gone 3.30 when I was to have the only run of the day. Again it was the close-in fished eel doing the business, it turning out to be yet another twenty pounder 20lbs 8oz.

It was the 24-12-2002 Christmas Eve, I wasn't going to go over to the pit, but I wanted to top up the swim with more bait, just in-case I didn't get the chance over the Christmas holidays. Also I have had some really good days in the past on Christmas Eve. Putting the rods in the car I tell Sheila I will only fish for a couple of hours. Roy couldn't make it as he had to do the Christmas shopping. Arriving on the pit the rods are cast out in double quick time. As I am fitting up the landing net the Mackerel tail's away within minutes of casting, 21lbs 12oz. As I am weighing her Ernie turns up and takes a photo. At 12 o'clock I am thinking of calling it a day, when the same rod with the mackerel on roars off. It is a big fish and it's going potty in the edge, as I try to wiggle it into the net. Out on the bank I recognise her right away, it's the 33lbs 8oz pike I caught eight days ago. The same fish Roy had next day at 34lbs 8oz. Checking her weight on the scales she goes 33lbs 12oz, dropping 12ozs but 4ozs heavier than when I had caught her last. As I let her slip back into the water, I am thinking to myself if I am lucky enough to catch her again, say in two months, she may weigh 35 pounds plus. So in a period of just six days on the pit, I have been very lucky to have caught four different twenties and a big thirty twice. Making all the baiting up worthwhile, it worked a treat. Drawing the pike from all over the pit to the baited area, and holding them there for weeks.

My last day on the pit in March 2003, just before the pike season finished was a strange session. At 7.30 I had a run on sardine and as I netted a nice pike, two others followed it into the net. So I hooked the scales into the net and weighed the three together, 38lbs, the biggest one 21lbs 2oz. At 1 o clock I have another double on sink and draw eel tail, and four more small fish. The pike obviously were starting to spawn, so I turned my attention to some carp that were moving in the reeds. Dropping a lump of crust among them, I hooked a 19lbs common within seconds, what a day.

With the pike season finished until October, I have a few weeks rest before bringing out the carp gear. My summers are normally spent stalking fish, not too seriously though. It's just good fun to walk around the lakes, picking off a surface feeding carp or the odd bubbler.

It was in the summer of 2003 that Sheila and I had decided to retire to Norfolk. I was surprised that Sheila had agreed, she hadn't been too keen in the past. So I booked my summer holidays, the first week at Pontins at Hemsby, second at Gunston Hall near Lowestoft. Using both destinations as a base, to search and explore for our new house. The first property we check out is a thatched cottage, situated just outside of Filby. As we walk up the path to the cottage, I pick up a peacocks feather lying in the grass. Looking up there is another one stuck in the thatch. The feathers were coming from the Thrigby wildlife centre next door. What a magnificent location and cottage, I could have moved in there and then. With Filby broad just down the road, and an endless supply of free peacock floats it would have been heaven. Unfortunately for me Sheila wasn't impressed, not being able to drive she felt the cottage was a bit isolated. We then check out Blofield, Great Plumstead, and Brundall, that will do for me, having the River Yare on my doorstep. Again it was a no, no, no with Sheila. The third day I pull up outside an estate agents in Acle. As I leave the car Sheila hasn't moved, "You coming inside?" I asked.

"No I don't want to move now," she replied.

She had reconsidered and changed her mind about moving, not wanting to be far away from the Grandchildren. The following week we still go to Gunston. However, the trip wasn't a complete waste of time as I have six big eels out on small dead baits in Gunston Hall's lake.

With the move to Norfolk on hold, for the time being, I turn my attention to the coming pike season. As the time is running out for these old bones of mine, I decide to have one more exerted effort on the big trout reservoirs. Nigel Williams has been good enough to hold a place for me on his pike syndicate water at Blithfield reservoir, also Ladybower (Masons) would be opening up. Chew Valley, I decide to give a miss this year because of the fly fishing for the pike in the summer. Grafham, Pitsford and the rest would have to wait hopefully for another time. So I will be concentrating on catching one last biggie, in Staffordshire and Derbyshire. Steve and I applied for tickets for Ladybower, and we were lucky to secure the first two days, plus some more two day sessions in the later months.

So how did I get on, it was a bloody disaster, almost a complete failure. The 11-12 of October 2003 were my first two days on Blithfield with Jason Davis my boat partner. On the way to the reservoir Jason is telling me about his last two years fishing the place, and all the big fish out. What a disappointment it was on seeing the water, well down and full of green algae. With the boats loaded up I didn't fancy our chances much. On the off, most of the boats raced across to watery lane, and start to whip the water to foam with lures. After an hour or two Jason managed to hook up a low double. With the sun high in the sky, and as the day progressed, with very little wind it got quite hot for the time of year. As the boats drifted away from watery lane an ice cream van turned up. So ends my first day on Blithfield with Jason and I sitting in the middle of the reservoir in just our t-shirts eating ice cream. My second day was no better, as we spent most of the day trolling lures around the reservoir. Then up and down the lines of barley straw that have been put there to combat the algae problem. It was along the bales of straw that I was to hook my first fish from Blithfield, a dead perch fowl hooked on a bulldawg. Later that day there were rumours of another dead perch and a trout hooked up from the bottom, not a good sign.

The 25-26 October 2003, saw my second two day session on Blithfield and the bright green algae had now gone brown. I found when retrieving my lures if they touched the bottom, the lure would be covered in a thick slime. I can sum up the fishing for the two days in one word, crap. Mind you I believe there were two twenties out, perhaps it was me and another 60 anglers who were not quite good enough in the diabolical conditions.

At the beginning of November I have a day on the River Yare with Steve. We had to work hard to catch a few baits in the heavy rain, giving us only a couple of hours trolling on the river. At 3.30 I am lucky to have a 20lbs 8oz fish after two jacks. It felt good to have a decent pike on the end of the rod again, after struggling on the trout reservoir. Steve went on to catch a 22lbs 8oz pike at the death. Steve's fish would be easy to recognise again having a lump the size of a tennis ball by the tail.

On the 8th November, most of the lads have booked up the Derwent Arms in Bamford, a couple of minutes drive from Ladybower reservoir. After a nice dinner we have one or two drinks before retiring to our beds, well some of us do. Apparently a bit of a drinking contest takes place, ending with Nige dancing on the tables before disappearing to be sick for the rest of the night. This left my mate Tony Corless to watch dave Kelbrick slowly sink under the table to cuddle a chair. Tony reckons the northern lads were light weights in the drinking stakes. Next morning checking out the reservoir we find it 40 feet down. It looked as good as Nige did in the half light, a bit the worse for wear. Picking up some trout Steve and I loaded up the boat and headed out to explore the water. Starting down the snake arm we find the water the colour of tea, with all the rain the day before. The wind was blowing hard across the end of the arm, making trolling difficult. We had to plot up for most of the morning. With no signs of a fish we headed back towards the main body of water, passing Jason Davis as we did so. Jason shouted across telling us he had just caught a 23lbs. I finally opened my account with a 12 pounder off the dam wall on a spring dawg. The second day of the session Steve and I blanked, but Jason went on to take what was to be the best fish from the pike trials on Ladybower that first year. Steve and I were trolling close along the bank of the reservoir opposite the fishery office. Steve cast out a lure and snagged the bank. As we go to retrieve it, Jason who was following us, trolled by. Then 30 yards further along the bank Jason gets a pull, the rest is history, 29lbs 8 oz well done mate.

There were about seven twenties out in all on the second day, Gary Banks and Kev Shore catching most of them. Gary having three twenties (greedy sod) and Kev landing one twenty. Steve and I like most of the other boats had struggled in the coloured water. That second day of the first session, turned out to be the best of the whole event.

The 22-23 November 2003 were my second two days on Ladybower. Right from the off I had a good double on a spring dawg in the main body of the reservoir, unhooking it the tail was missing from the lure. (anyone want to buy 75 quids worth of tail-less spring dawgs). Later in the day fishing close to raspberry bay, both Steve and I pull off a couple of good fish. Only having big baits, a pound plus trout, we found the pike were throwing the baits in the fight. Second day out we head straight to where we had lost the fish the day before. After two hours without a run we decide to troll on down towards snake river. At long last we start to put some fish in the boat, Steve having a big double, then I had a double and a small one. As we swing round to come back up the arm, we see Chris Turnball's boat partner playing a fish which went 23lbs. Fifty yards further along the bank in 18 feet of water one of my floats disappears, pulling into the fish it feels big. Two minutes later the pike's on the surface, and I start to worry in case she throws the hooks. Steve makes no mistakes with the net, peering in it looks like a mid-twenty, on the scales 26lbs. After eight days hard fishing I have finally caught a decent pike from the trout reservoirs.

It's three weeks before I am back fishing at Ladybower, so I spend some

Who wants to buy some tailess hungry Dawgs?

Ladybower 26lbs.

time on my local waters. With all the travelling up to Staffordshire and Derbyshire, (over 400 miles round trip) even the rivers of Norfolk, (200 miles), it was nice to be able to get up at a reasonable hour, and still be on the water before first light. As it happened, the piking on one of my waters was on fire. Only being able to fish for a couple of hours before or after work, depending on shifts it was terrific. In fact it was so good I even managed to reach a milestone in my pike fishing, catching my 200th twenty. The pike coming on the 30-11-2003. I was fishing with Steve and we had already caught a number of fish, including some nice doubles. When I had a run on a polyed live roach, it turned out to be a 25lbs 4oz fish, well pleased.

On 6-7 December 2003 I am back on the M1 heading north to Ladybower, for another two-day session. First morning Steve and I head down to the very end of the snake arm, and within minutes I pull out of two fish on the big baits again. I just can't seem to get a good hook hold, even though I am using 3 hook rigs now. Steve did manage to land a 16lb. Later in the day we went back to cover the same area again, Steve had his second double and I pull out of another one (I can't print what I said!). Next day we go back to the snake arm, I have a small double and Steve missed out. We decide to call it a day and go home early, what with the long drive. I was told later that there wasn't too much caught over the two days, it's not looking good for the very big pike.

Our next and last two day session on Ladybower was on the 10-11 January. First morning Steve had two nice big doubles, I just managed a jack not much bigger than the bait. At the end of the day we retired back to the Derwent arms, for dinner a drink and bed. After dinner some of the northern lads joined us in the lounge for a drink. It wasn't too long before the banter was flying about, what with one or two comedians among us, all in good fun though. Talking of comedians I thought Tony Cookney was a dead ringer for Bobby ball, out of Cannon and Ball. Then there was a laugh a minute Kevin Beasley, I am sure Kevin could make a living on the stage.

With all the good company it was late when Steve and I staggered to our beds. Getting up the next morning Steve didn't look too good, in fact he looked terrible. Loading up the boat with the tackle I noticed he had gone from white to a shade of yellow. Pulling away from the bank I opened up the outboard motor, making the boat jump up and down across the waves. Steve started to give me the impression he was now turning into the incredible hulk, going a bright green. Three hours later we have packed up and I am now driving him home, he wants to die in Essex, so ends our time on Ladybower reservoir.

It's another six weeks before I have my last two days on Blithfield, so I make hay in the meanwhile, taking four twenties from the rivers and the gravel pits, two of which go over 25 pounds. But all too soon I am on my way with Jason back to Staffordshire. We are hoping Blithfield will at last give up one or two of her big pike. We were late as we loaded our gear into the boat off the jetty, Mick Brown and Dave Kelbrick were already motoring away at full speed, still keen I think to myself. But I was wrong, still on the jetty were Micks rods, obviously he didn't fancy his chances that much, not bothering taking his rods out with him!

Anyway back to the fishing, it was in the very last hour on my last day I was to have my only pull on the reservoir, the shock nearly giving me a heart attack. One minute the rod's bent over and thumping away, then suddenly the rod is limp, the bloody pike is off. My total catch on Blithfield for eight days hard fishing, one small dead perch foul hooked.

To sum up my time on the two reservoirs, with the very low water and the algae problem, the pike have probably suffered big time. Ladybower was not a complete disaster as I did have one decent fish from there. I should have been on them a couple of years earlier, it could be a few years before the fishing is back to its best. Unfortunately I probably have not the years left to wait. The only trout water to fish well was the Chew Valley, with seven pike over 30 pounds caught. The one I decided to give a miss, you win some and lose some.

Well that's me nearly up to date on my fishing, since I wrote the original 'Dimples to Wrinkles' back in 1997. In the last entry in my diary as I write, Steve and I have had a blinding day and a half on the Yare. On our return from Ireland we had gone down for a bit of fishing and also to take one of the boats out on the river, to use on the broads for a weeks holiday. I had lost count of the number of pike we caught that weekend. Unfortunately we had to forgo the landing net, having left it in the van. With fish weighing up to 24lbs 14oz, having to hand everyone out was a bit hairy to say the least. Steve's hand was in quite a state by the end of the day. I am definitely losing the plot, what with going out without the net, Steve and I set up a photo shoot, the boat's cleaned up Steve one end with three cameras ready, me at the other end with the pike. I turn the fish to get the best side, then like a bar of soap she shot straight out of my arms back into the river.

My 200th twenty 25lbs 4oz.

What of the future, do we at times take our piking all too seriously?

A couple of years ago Dave Horton wrote an article in pike and Predators, called x-men and the x-factor. It was about why do a small number of anglers catch more and bigger pike than others. In the following publication of the magazine, Phil Wakeford had responded to Dave's article in the letter page. To cut a long story short, towards the end of Phil's letter he wrote: "after all, as Bill Palmer put it, a pike is only a bit of wet fish that we are after and it's important to have other interests and loves in life in order to retain one's sanity and keep things like catching fish in some sort of perspective."

Well I don't know if I actually put it like that, I might have said "If a pike was a cod we would be eating it with chips."

Anyway I showed Phil's letter to Sheila, her reaction shocked me. I thought I was more laid back with my piking now. After all the years I have been fishing for them, and the big fish I have caught. After getting the same reaction from a few friends, I thought do I still take my fishing too seriously? Well I don't know much about the x-men, but over time I have been told on many occasions I have a nose to sniff out the big pike. As my tally of big pike has increased over time, so has the size of my nose. It eventually got so big I finally just had to have an operation to reduce it. Would my smaller nose still work? Is it my x-factor, I thought to myself? Well I don't know if it is my x-factor, but I found a little bit of Max-factor to hide the damage on my nose didn't go amiss. Joking apart though, a young angler taking up pike fishing today may find it a bit daunting. Not only has he got to learn how to handle and unhook pike safely. But after reading about hot spots, feeding times, weather conditions, barometric pressures, and my favourite, moon phases, he then finds on the only day a week he is able to fish, the weather's against him, the barometric pressure is too high, and the moon is in the wrong quarter. He probably feels defeated before he starts. Sure it's important, but it's not the end of the world. Let's just lighten up a bit, smell the roses along the way and enjoy our great sport.

Talking of lightening up, I would like to finish by going back to the Derwent Arms in Derbyshire, when the northern lads had joined us for a drink in the lounge. Kev Beasley who was sitting next to me, stood up and said in a loud voice, "Bill you have let me down."

"I have let you down mate, what do you mean?" I replied,

A big twenty with a yellow head one side.

Who takes their piking too seriously. Give us a kiss!!

"I am very disappointed, I had picked you in a dead mans raffle." He said to sounds of laughter.

Well Kev, let's hope it's a few more years and pike before you collect mate.

11

THE 2004 - 2005 SEASON
(THE OAP YEARS...)

AS I finish my update to this book I must tell you about the 2004-05 season. I don't want to brag but this has been one magical season; you just could not make it up. A few years back having had a good start to my piking, I tried to catch twenty, twenties in a season. I came very close a couple of times, missing out with 19 fish.

The season started very well and by the end of the year I am on 12 twenties. A great start but now things get very interesting. On the 31 December, the last day of the year I am fishing an Essex lake and at midday I have lovely marked 26lbs 2oz. Four days later I have a 21lb from a large gravel pit. Five days on, on the 9 January I am in Norfolk and catch another three twenties on the day weighing 24lbs 10oz, 24lbs, and 21lbs. Now anyone would be more than satisfied with a catch like that what with 3 twenties in a day. But it was to get even better, a brace from another gravel pit, weighing 24lbs and 21lbs 8 oz on the 13 January; this puts me on 19 for the season.

A couple of days later on the 15 January I am in Lincolnshire to fish a water I have not been back to for two years. I am fishing with Steve Wells and Roy Lyons; with tongue in cheek I tell them just the one twenty will do me today for my twentieth twenty. It's late in the day and I have not had a run when one of my dead bait rods is away. I pick up the rod and feeling down discover the pike's dropped the bait. So I cast a float fished roach right over the dead bait to see if the pike would still like to play. Instantly the float disappeared and I am playing a big fish. After a few heart-stopping moments Steve slipped the net under a 32lbs 10oz monster. So in just five days fishing in the New Year I had already reached my goal with a bloody big thirty. With still eight weeks of the season to go, I have made my target having

225

caught 113 doubles and twenty, twenties. With the twenties coming from eight different venues. But that's not the end the fishing just gets better.

Six days on I am fishing a gravel pit in the southeast that I have been baiting up hard and have another unbelievable day. I catch three twenties weighing 20lbs 8oz, 20lbs 12oz, and 21lbs plus a double. It's the second time this season I have been lucky to have caught three twenties in a day, and coming from two different waters in Norfolk and Essex I'm well pleased.

On the 1st Febuary I am back over the gravel pit I had the three twenties from, and have another brace of twenties and a small double. As I mentioned earlier I have been baiting the gravel pit up heavily every 3-4 days for months, throwing the bait in when I finished fishing. I leave the rods out to the last bombarding the floats with the pre-bait, as the water rocked around the floats I had a run resulting in one of the twenties. It's the second time I have had a run when throwing the pre-bait around the floats at the end of my fishing. It seems the pike have learned the bombardment of bait going in for months has become their dinner bell, bringing them into the area to feed. So I start to put half the pre-bait in at the beginning of my sessions, it normally results in a fish within minutes. After an hour or so if I have had no more runs I will then throw another half a dozen 2 inch size lumps of pre-bait again around the floats. A lot of the time the bait going in results in another quick fish. I do believe the pike attracted to the baited area are now competing for the pre-bait as it's thrown in.

Anyway back to the fishing. Two days after my brace from the gravel pit, I am fishing the Warren in Essex and have a 24lbs 10oz on my only run of the day. Five days later I am back over the baited gravel pit and catch a 21lbs 8oz first cast, after throwing in half the pre-bait. At the end of the day and with no more runs to the rods, I start throwing the rest of the pre-bait around the floats again resulting in a run almost immediately, 25lbs 4oz it's yet another brace for me. Three days later I am back to top up the swim with more bait, I only fished for a couple of hours but still managed to have a dropped run and net another twenty, 20lbs 8oz. Four days on it's 15 February and I am back on the pit again putting half the pre-bait in from the off. Before I can cast my second rod out the first rod's away, a nice double. An hour later I start bombarding the floats with another couple of pounds of pre-bait. I have only thrown about half in when one of the floats disappeared. Unfortunately as I go to net a good pike it spits the mackerel right back at me. Checking the bait and hooks are all right I cast it back out into the baited area. The bait

226

My Thirtieth Twenty of the Season 26lb 4oz

can only have just reached bottom, when the float shot under and the pike's taking line. I pull into the fish and a couple of minutes later I slipped the net under a lovely conditioned pike weighing 26lbs 4oz. This is my thirtieth twenty of the season and it's come only a month after I had achieved my twenty twenties ambition.

Three days later after blanking in Norfolk apart from a small jack, I have another twenty from my baited pit of 22 pounds. Then on the 20 February the weather turns very cold; it even started to snow when fishing the warren with Steve. With six rods out between us we didn't have a run. For the next couple of weeks the lakes were partly frozen over for most of the time and the fishing has become very hard. I only managed to get out once or twice for very little.

Then with just a week of the pike season left, the weather started to pick up, and I am back over my baited pit. The margins are still iced up, but are melting quite quickly as the temperature starts to rise. Throwing half my pre-bait in I have a 6lb and 17lb within minutes. I am only fishing the morning so an hour later I throw the last of the pre-bait around the floats resulting in a 20lbs 4oz. Two days later I am back on the pit for the last time

My 3rd Twenty of the Day in Norfolk

before the season finishes. Catching a 12 pound fish from the off, then at 10.45 after putting more bait around the floats my sardines away and I go on to land my best pike so far from the pit, 27lbs.

On my last day of the season I decide to check out Ardleigh reservoir, right down the end of the west arm to see if the pike have moved down there before spawning.

Arriving at the end of the reservoir the water is the colour of tea. The water company having cut and dragged out all the trees and bushes from the water. So I give the reservoir a miss and move on to a couple of lakes in Norfolk. The first is full up with match and pleasure anglers. The second has bivvys set up all around the lake, the carp boys doing the last few days of the season. Back in the car I head for the cut off channel, with only half the day left and doing over 100 miles I finally cast a paternostered roach out. Before I can cast my second rod the first's away, pulling into the fish it feels heavy as it takes line. Surfacing it looked a good twenty, slipping the landing net into the water the pike kicks and it's gone. Well you can't win them all. Three hours later with eight fish up to 17 pounds and a few missed chances the bait runs out and I am on my way home.

So there you have it my first season pike fishing as an old aged pensioner, and what a season I have had I should have retired years ago. Age being no barrier to success in this wonderful sport of ours; let's hope it's not my swan song.

The Icing on the Cake, 32lbs 10oz Fen Pike

I finished this magical season having caught 134 doubles, 33 twenties and a thirty. Five braces of twenties and three in a day, twice on two different waters. The thirty being my tenth and coming from the fens was the icing on the cake.

This wrinkled old aged pensioner has been on fire, in fact I am SMOKING!!!

12

CONCLUSION

So the deed is re-done, warts and all; I trust that you have enjoyed its pages and that it will encourage you to get out on to the bank. In retrospect I could have written more about rigs and methods, but most of it has been said before a million times. I wanted to highlight particular favourite methods of mine, the ones which have brought me most success over the years. Yet there is not a lot more one can say about a piece of wire and a couple of trebles. My best advice is to keep rigs as simple as you can and don't complicate things for the sake of it.

I have often been asked what is the secret of catching big pike, but really there is no secret. Big pike are not that difficult to catch and I can sum it all up into just one word - location.

Having said that, there is a catch - to achieve consistent success you must spend time on the water and the more time the better. If I had used just half the time and energy I have spent on the bank after pike, trying to make money instead of fishing, I could have retired years ago. There is no way that I would change a second of it however! I'd do it all again. Do remember though, fishing is all about enjoyment; don't let it become too heavy and end up like a work substitute.

The Warren fish came as a big shock to me, and I'll bet there are still a lot of anglers who remain sceptical, and I couldn't blame them. If I hadn't been personally involved and had not cradled her in my own arms I have to admit, I too would probably have my doubts. As time passed even I started to think that it was all a dream, then just recently Mick Toomer, who had the pike set up, invited me to his home to be reunited with the big girl. As I caught sight of her on Mick's lounge wall the memory of that fateful day came flooding back. There is only one word to describe her, she is awesome. Hopefully, in the near future I will have a cast of that great pike so there will be an open invitation to all pike anglers to see this monster for themselves.

Ardleigh reservoir. What a fantastic water it is and one which has proven to be one of this country's top pike fisheries of the 1990's. It keeps doing the business, year after year. As I was putting the final touches to the original book I was to catch my first pike over 35lbs, and that too came from Ardleigh reservoir. A tremendously long fish for a trout water pike weighing 36lbs 8ozs and 48.5 inches long and 24.5 inches in girth. Oh for another couple of inches on her girth!

Who is complaining? I'm not and there is always tomorrow. Thank God for tomorrow!

Good luck to you all.

Bill Palmer.